Sudha KU- 627 -659

Child of the Divide

D1364861

Bloomsbury Methuen Drama
An imprint of Bloomsbury Publishing Plc

Bloomsbury Methuen Drama
An imprint of Bloomsbury Publishing Plc

Imprint previously known as Methuen Drama

50 Bedford Square	1385 Broadway
London	New York
WC1B 3DP	NY 10018
UK	USA

www.bloomsbury.com

**BLOOMSBURY, METHUEN DRAMA and the Diana logo
are trademarks of Bloomsbury Publishing Plc**

First published by Methuen Drama, 2006

This edition published 2017

British Library Cataloguing-in-Publication Data
A catalogue record for this book is available from the British Library.

ISBN: PB: 978-1-3500-5940-5
ePDF: 978-1-3500-5941-2
eBook: 978-1-3500-5942-9

Library of Congress Cataloging-in-Publication Data
A catalog record for this book is available from the Library of Congress.

Series: Modern Plays

Cover design: Olivia d'Cruz

Typeset by Mark Heslington Ltd, Scarborough, North Yorkshire
Printed and bound in Great Britain

Bhuchar Boulevard

Bhuchar Boulevard is founded by acclaimed theatre maker and actor Sudha Bhuchar, to create unforgettable theatre for multiple and diverse audiences by holding up a mirror to our common humanity.

Bhuchar Boulevard projects will be inspired by and inform Sudha Bhuchar's evolving practice and build on her canon of ground-breaking, landmark work.

These will be made and curated through creative dialogue and collaboration with artist associates; arts and not-arts partners, communities and audiences – displaying an empathetic approach and an ability to be at home with culturally and politically sensitive stories in all their complexity.

With a great emphasis on research and excavating personal and intimate stories of lives that take unexpected and diverse directions; Bhuchar Boulevard will paint a broader canvas of today's changing world through capturing the cultural hybridity inherent in our everyday lives.

The hallmark of Bhuchar Boulevard is a lightness of touch that is emotional yet intelligent; truthful and innovative; heartfelt and humorous.

This timely revival of *Child of the Divide* invites a public conversation around the lost narratives of children and marks the launch of Bhuchar Boulevard. Other projects in development include *Golden Hearts* (a personal look at the inheritance of loss in Asian families from heart disease).

www.bhucharboulevard.com
@BhucharBvrd
www.facebook.com/BhucharBoulevard

The Partition History Project

Seventy years on, the terrible suffering and loss at the time of the Partition is still a taboo subject in Britain. This brave play bears testimony to the consequences of political and interfaith failure on the life of one child. Having staged *Child of the Divide* for Luton and Hitchin school children, as part of a pilot to model teaching the history of Partition in schools, I have seen at first hand the effect on a whole variety of people.

All seemed to emerge emotionally wiser, more compassionate, more determined to celebrate and build what we have in common across faith lines. This was not merely my opinion. In the comprehensive evaluation by the Runnymede Trust on the project there was a clear verdict. This play aids compassion between people of different faiths.

The Partition Project was started by clergy friends (Michael Roden, Martin Henwood and Ed Probert) who came across the legacy of distrust dating from the Indian Partition in their interfaith work and wished to positively address this. The Project aims to explore and model methods to teach the Partition well in a whole variety of media in a way that will build greater understanding between faith communities.

Michael Roden
www.partitionhistoryproject.com
@PartitionHProj

Polka Theatre

Polka is one of the few theatres in the UK dedicated exclusively to young audiences aged 0–12. Based in Wimbledon since 1979, Polka gives children from all backgrounds the opportunity to experience thrilling, innovative, world-class theatre. Every year it welcomes over 90,000 children, parents and teachers to an exciting range of productions, from the vibrant and sensory musical, *Hatch*, for ages 2–5 (a co-commission and co-production with The Royal Opera), to the world premiere of *Child of the Divide* in 2006 (a co-production with Tamasha theatre company), now re-staged to mark the 70th anniversary of Partition. With a thriving creative learning programme, workshops, storytelling sessions and a café, playground and garden, there are always opportunities at Polka for children to play, laugh, discover and create in a welcoming space that they can call their own.

www.polkatheatre.com
@polkatheatre

The Big Imaginations Festival

The Big Imaginations Festival is a two-week celebration of the best in theatre for children and families. Programmed by the Big Imaginations network of fifteen venues across the North West, they share a commitment to bringing brilliant children's theatre to audiences that otherwise wouldn't have such opportunity. The Big Imaginations network is led by Z-arts, Manchester's venue for children and families.

In October 2017 Big Imaginations are taking nine brilliant shows across 26 venues in the North West including Greater Manchester, Lancashire, Cheshire and Merseyside, and now expanding into Yorkshire. All the work is programmed to reflect the diversity of modern family life in the UK, with a rich mix of shows with music, dance and stories from all over the world. Every venue will also run art cart activities, outreach workshops and numerous ways for families to engage with the festival to inspire lasting relationships with the venues in their communities.

www.bigimaginations.co.uk
@BImaginations

Cast and Creatives

Cast

Karan Gill	Pali
Halema Hussain	Zainab/Hasina
Devesh Kishore	Shakur/Pagal Head
Nyla Levy	Kaushalya/Aisha
Diljohn Singh	Manohar Lal/Buttameez

Creatives

Writer	Sudha Bhuchar
Director	Jim Pope
Designer	Sue Mayes
Composer/Sound Designer	Arun Ghosh
Lighting Designer	Peter Harrison
Movement Director	Deborah Galloway
Production Manager	Denis Charles
Assistant Director	Emily Aboud
Stage Manager	Ben Jones
Stage Manager	Vicky Jukes
Wardrobe	Annie James
Casting Director	Emily Jones

For Bhuchar Boulevard

Artistic Director/Producer	Sudha Bhuchar
Producer	Dan Coleman
Communications Consultant	Suman Bhuchar
Press and PR	David Burns
Marketing & Advertising	JHI Marketing

Thanks To:
Michael Roden, Sarah Ansari, Martin Henwood, Ed Probert, Valerie Synmoie,
Alex Towers and the team at Tamasha theatre company, The Runnymede Trust,
Elizabeth Jeanes, Fiona Razvi and Wimbledon Bookfest, Anita Rani, Claire
Alexander, Jenny Killick, Rachel Parslew, Stephen Moran, Catherine Gibbs

Sudha Bhuchar – Writer

Sudha is an actor/playwright and co-founder of Tamasha theatre company where she served as co-artistic director for 26 years. She has written extensively for Tamasha and her landmark plays include *Fourteen Songs, Two Weddings and a Funeral* (winner of Barclays/ TMA Best Musical), an adaptation of *A Fine Balance*, by Rohinton Mistry, and *Strictly Dandia* (all with Kristine Landon-Smith). Her solo plays include *The House of Bilquis Bibi* (Lorca's *The House of Bernada Alba* transposed to contemporary Pakistan) and the critically acclaimed *My Name is...* which she also adapted for Radio 4, where it was 'pick of the week'.

Sudha's extensive acting career includes *East Enders, Doctors* and *Casualty* for the BBC, *Stella* for Sky TV, and she played Sonia Rahman in *Coronation Street*. Theatre credits include many plays at Tamasha; *Khandan*, by Gurpreet Bhatti (Birmingham Rep and Royal Court); and most recently *Lions and Tigers* by Tanika Gupta (Globe Theatre). Sudha is a regular contributor on Radio 4, where she also currently under co-commission with Saleyha Ahsan. She is also part of an exciting international collaboration lead by National Theatre Wales called *Sisters*. Sudha will make her first Disney appearance in *Mary Poppins Returns* in December 2018.

Suman Bhuchar – Communications Consultant

Suman Bhuchar works in arts promotion and production. She began as an actor at Tara Arts, then moved to press and marketing working with Tamasha, Kali, Motiroti and Tara. She has worked on flagship projects with mainstream companies including The Really Useful Group, Royal Shakespeare Company and Watermans. Recent credits include: Phizzical Productions (*Bring on the Bollywood*); Ambassadors Theatre Group (*East is East*, 2014/15); Amina Khayyam Dance Company and Bhuchar Boulevard. She is interested in contributing to creating a cultural landscape that respects artists from BAME sector and is an advocate for the same. @SumanBhuchar

David Burns – Press & PR

After training as an actor at Rose Bruford, David moved into arts and entertainment press and publicity. His twenty-five-year career has included in-house press and marketing roles at Rambert Dance Company, Avalon, Wall To Wall Television, The Really Useful Group and The Society of London Theatre. David set up his own company in 2002. David Burns PR has a diverse range of clients both in the commercial and subsidised sectors as well individuals. These include include Harry Shearer, Actors Touring Company, Nottingham Playhouse, Told By An Idiot, Jasmin Vardimon Dance Company, Jermyn Street Theatre and The Marlowe Theatre Canterbury.

Dan Coleman – Producer

Dan is the artistic director and producer of Dawn State Theatre Company (dawnstate.co.uk). Credits for the company include *The Wonderful Discovery of Witches in the County of Lancaster* (New Diorama & Greenwich Theatre, 2016; Oxford Playhouse & Edinburgh Festival, 2015) and *The Man Who Would Be King* (UK tour, 2016; New Diorama & Edinburgh Festival, 2014). Other producing credits include *Skittles* (BAC & Edinburgh Festival, 2012; BBC Radio 4, 2013); *Urban Scrawl* (Theatre503/Latitude Festival, 2009) and, as associate producer: *My Name is...* (Edinburgh & Scottish tour, 2015) and *Blood* (UK tour, 2015) for Tamasha. He was the joint programming director at Theatre503 (2009) and the recipient of the TDA emerging producer bursary at Tamasha theatre company (2015). He trained at Birkbeck College.

Deborah Galloway – Movement Director

Deborah Galloway is a freelance choreographer and movement director currently working on *Jekyll & Hyde* for the National Youth Theatre Rep Company, performing at The Ambassadors Theatre, London, this autumn. Recently Deborah choreographed *Hacienda Paradise* for Inner Ground Dance Company, which performed at the Elixir Festival, Sadler's Wells, and as a Curtain Raiser for Rambert's tour at Hall for Cornwall, Truro 2017.

In 2016 Deborah was Associate Director for the National Theatre performance *We're Here Because We're Here*, a UK-wide public event commissioned by 14–18 NOW to commemorate the Battle of the Somme, in the Second World War.

Arun Ghosh – Composer/Sound Designer

Arun Ghosh is a clarinettist, composer and music educator. Recent credits include *Lions and Tigers* (Shakespeare's Globe); *Made in India* and *My Name Is . . .* (Tamasha). Winner of 'Jazz Instrumentalist of the Year' at the 2014 Parliamentary Jazz Awards, Ghosh is a leading light on the UK and international jazz scenes.

A renowned innovator of the modern IndoJazz style, his critically acclaimed albums are: *Northern Namaste* (2008), *Primal Odyssey* (2011) and *A South Asian Suite* (2013). Arun composed the score for the original production of *Child of the Divide* and has been delighted to revisit his music to this wonderful play.

Peter Harrison – Lighting Designer

Peter trained at RADA.

Recent lighting designs include *Julius Caesar* (Guildford Shakespeare Company), *The Cardinal* (Southwark Playhouse), *Pink Mist* (Bristol Old Vic), Paper Cinema's *Macbeth* and *Alfie White: Space Explorer* (Tall Stories).

Other lighting designs: *Much do About Nothing* (Ludlow Festival), *Jerry's Girls* (St. James Theatre), *Orestes* (Shared Experience), *Translunar Paradise* (Theatre Ad Infinitum), *The Doubtful Guest* (Hoipolloi) and *Wuthering Heights* (Tamasha).

Opera and dance credits: *Paul Bunyan* (Welsh National Youth Opera), *Opera Works* (ENO Baylis), *In Nocentes* and *Home Turf* (Sadler's Wells), and *Jean and Antonin* (Gartnerplatz, Munich).

Other work as an Associate Lighting Designer includes *Collaborators* and *As You Like It* (National Theatre), *Made in Dagenham* (Adelphi Theatre) and *The Commitments* (Palace Theatre, London).

Ben Jones – Stage Manager

Benedict Jones trained at the Bristol Old Vic Theatre School in Stage Management. He is a prolific touring Stage Manager, travelling and working throughout the UK. Theatre credits include: Company Stage Manager for Changeling Theatre's tours of *All's Well That Ends Well*, *She Stoops to Conquer* and *Hamlet* (South

East Tours). Stage Manager for *Roundelay* (Southwark Playhouse), *And Then Come the Nightjars* (Bristol Old Vic, Theatre503, Perth Theatre), *Shot at Dawn* (South West Tour), *Nutshell Nutcracker* (Tropicana), *Disco Pigs* (National Tour), *Edmund the Learned Pig* (National Tour), *Animals* (Theatre503), *Walking The Chains* (The Passenger Shed, Bristol), *Stardust* (South West Tour).

Victoria Jukes – Stage Manager

Vicky has had a varied theatre career since training at Guildford School of Acting, from director to choreographer, actress to stage manager. She is currently resident DSM for Yvonne Arnaud Theatre and PPA Drama School in Guildford, and for the last three years has been CSM for Story Pocket Theatre Company. Aside from a stage management career she also teaches and choreographs for The Oxford Academy of Dance and First Dance Studios. Recent touring has included *The Man Who Would Be King* for Dawn State. *Child of the Divide* is her debut production with Bhuchar Boulevard.

JHI Marketing – Marketing and Advertising

JHI is an independently owned, dedicated and passionate team of arts marketing professionals who have been operating since 2009.

They provide a wide range of marketing services offering truly personal and bespoke campaigns. JHI are delighted to be working with Bhuchar Boulevard on this beautiful production. The marketing creative was designed by Rebecca Pitt Creative in conjunction with JHI.

Sue Mayes – Designer

Sue Mayes has a long and varied career as a designer and teacher. Her work stretches from pantomime and Young People's Theatre to film and corporate work. After obtaining an Honours Degree from the Central School of Art and Design, she began her professional career in traditional British repertory theatre in Ipswich, then moved into devised theatre at The Belgrade Theatre in Education Company. Since then Sue has worked with many different theatre companies such as the Theatre Royal Stratford East, Derby Playhouse and especially for Tamasha, having designed all their major productions up to 2001, including the original design for the *Child of the Divide* premiere in 2006. She particularly enjoys designing for new writing and devised work.

Jim Pope – Director

Jim Pope is a director, actor and teacher.

He set up the level 3 accredited Playing Up programme for young people not in education, employment or training at the National Youth Theatre.

He has recently directed the Headz monologues for *20 Stories High* in Liverpool and national tour.

As co-artistic director of Playing ON Theatre Company he directed *Inside,* by Philip Osment at the Roundhouse, Camden, and is currently directing and acting in *Hearing Things* by Osment at Theatre Royal Stratford East and Birmingham Rep Theatre.

He specialises in social inclusion and has led programmes of work for Cardboard Citizens, Leap Confronting Conflict, Safe Ground and the Maudsley, working in prisons, hostels and psychiatric hospitals.

Emily Aboud – Assistant Director

Emily Aboud was born and raised in Trinidad and Tobago. She has just completed her MA in Theatre Directing from Mountview Academy of Theatre Arts. Recent directing credits include: *Fireworks* (Karamel Club) and *Spring Awakening* (Edinburgh Fringe 2016). Her assistant directing credits include *Deposit* (Hampstead Theatre) and *The Good Person of Szechuan* (Bridewell Theatre).

Emily Jones – Casting Director

Film and TV casting directors' credits include *Doctors* (BBC), *Beauty* (Moolmore Films), *What Happened to Evie* (French Fancy Productions), *Practice* (Deva Films), *Collection Only* (Constant Productions).

Theatre casting director credits include *Some Mothers Do 'Ve 'Em* (Limelight Productions), *PowerPlay* (Hampton Court), *Orca* (Southwark Playhouse), *Donkey Heart* (Trafalgar Studios/Old

Red Lion), *Coolatully* (Finborough), *World Enough & Time* (Park Theatre), *The Hard Man* (Finborough).

She has also worked with Ginny Schiller on various theatre projects including *The Father* (Bath & West End), *1984* (West End & tours) & *Bad Jews* (Bath & West End).

Cast

Karan Gill (Pali)

Training: Royal Central School of Speech and Drama.

Film: Rama in *Boogieman* (MGMM).

Roles whilst training: Dash in *A Serious Case of the F*ckits*; Spanish Gentleman in *The Heresy of Love.*

Other credits: *Sweet Love Remember'd* at Shakespeare's Globe; Claudio in *All Places That the Eye of Heaven Visits* at Shakespeare's Globe.

Halema Hussain (Zainab/Hasina)

A recent graduate from The Academy of Live and Recorded Arts, *Child of the Divide* marks Halema's professional debut.

Stage credits include: Mary Warren – *The Crucible* directed by Sean Turner; Lucy Morgan/Hamnet Shakespeare – *Shakespeare's Sister*, directed by Titania Krimpas; Maria – *The Funfair.*

Film credits include: *The Scar*, Noor Afshan Mirza and Brad Butler (HOME Artist Film & n.o.w.here, 2017), directed by Gary Sefon. Halema worked extensively with the Equity and Diversity Panel.

Devesh Kishore (Shakur/Pagal Head)

Credits include: Raj/Flavio, *Gangsta Granny*, directed by Neal Foster; Shakur/Pagal Head, *Child of the Divide*, directed by Jim Pope; Sami, *Piece of Silk*, directed by Tania Azevedo; Aditya, *Stowaway*, directed by Hannah Barker and Lewis Heatherington. Whilst training at the Royal Welsh College of Music and Drama: Roderigo, *Duchess of Malfi*, directed by Greg Hersov; *Ring Ring*, directed by Ned Bennett; Tartuffe, *Tartuffe*, directed by Jamie Garven; Antonio, *The Merchant of Venice*, directed by Simon Reeves.

Nyla Levy (Kaushalya/Aisha)

Theatre includes: *Different is Dangerous* (Two's Company/Theatre 503); Rima in *Street/Life* (Cardboard Citizens); Self in *Like Mother, Like Daughter* (Battersea Arts Centre); Storyteller in *100 Stories* (Hackney Empire); Kulli in *Punjabi Girl* (Rich Mix); Sameena in *The Rebel & The Runaway* (G.I.Y.P.T); *Yasmin* in *That Isis Play Innit!* (The Space); *Keywords* (Lyric Hammersmith); Rashida in *Homegrown: I am Taboo* (Battersea Arts Centre); Sheza in *Prevent Tours* (Pint Sized Theatre); Shaheeda in *The Diary of a Hounslow Girl* (National Tour); and most recently Aisha and Saima in *Magna Carter* (National Theatre Studio).

Film includes: Grace in *Personality Aid* (Nathan Cook), Mia in *Prevent* (CrisisCast), Mia in *Safeguarding* (CrisisCast), and Insta_Princess_xx in *Finding Fatima* (BMTV).

Television includes: Sophia in *Guiding Lights* (ITV Mammoth Screen).

Diljohn Singh (Manohar Lal/Buttameez)

Diljohn was born in India. He began as a model and actor in Mumbai and came to England to study at Birmingham School of Acting, graduating in 2014. He is a well-rounded actor with an incredible work ethic and is quite fearless on stage. He is a competent singer.

Theatre: *All's Well That Ends Well, Total Eclipse, Phaedra, In Extremis, Bedlam, Motortown, Water under the Bridge, Punjabi Girl, Punjabi Boy, Silent Sisters.*

Television: *Sanjay & Karishma, Agatha Raisin.*

Film: *The Hanged Man, The Last Good Bye, Home Office, Raagini, Aghori, Guest in London, Khido Khundi.*

 The National Archives

COMMEMORATING THE PARTITION OF BRITISH INDIA

As the British Government's official archive, The National Archives holds an important collection of records that contribute to our understanding of both the period before and after the Partition of British India. The National Archives has been actively engaged in commemorating the Partition of British India for some years now, launching an online education resource and in 2010 running the project 'Punjab 1947: A heart divided' that included interviewing four Partition survivors.

In 2017 – on the 70th anniversary of Partition – The National Archives' Outreach team is leading on an events, exhibitions and online programme, focusing on the planning for Partition and its devastating fallout. The opportunity in this anniversary year to collaborate with Bhuchar Boulevard and its new touring production of *Child of the Divide* is another example of our commitment to marking this momentous event in world history.

Iqbal Husain, Outreach and Learning Officer at The National Archives, said Sudha Bhuchar's play – based on Bhisham Sahni's short story – movingly portrays from the child's eye the story of Partition. Excellently woven within the script are numerous references to experiences that reflect records held at The National Archives. Spoken from characters who are children makes the violence and chaos of Partition so much more poignant and moving. Characters in the play point to the looting, ethnic cleansing, retribution and the extraordinary levels of displacement people experienced. These are real events found in official government records and corroborated by witnesses who experienced the events. Grounded in historical sources, this play is a creative and accessible way into a troubling history, offering space for reflection and in some cases, healing.

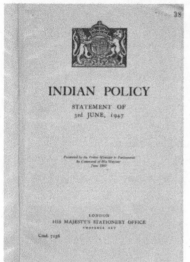

28

The Plan to Partition

The plan to partition British India into two new nation states – India and Pakistan – was announced in June 1947. The expected date of British withdrawal from India had been brought forward a whole year and attempts by leaders on all sides to find a compromise had broken down. The violence that ensued saw many millions made refugees and over a million dead.

Catalogue reference: PREM 8/541/10

Cabinet Papers May 1947

Shortly after being appointed Viceroy, Lord Mountbatten arrived in London seeking approval for a plan to partition British India and make final the departure of the British and the transfer of power. The plan was approved by the British Cabinet, with the caveat that robust action would need to be taken to stop excessive communal violence.

> (e) *The Prime Minister* said that communal feeling in India was now intense and it was possible that serious disorders might break out in the Punjab and certain other Provinces at any time after the announcement of the plan for partitioning India. It was the Viceroy's considered view that the only hope of checking widespread communal warfare was to suppress the first signs of it promptly and ruthlessly, using for this purpose all the force required, including tanks and aircraft, and giving full publicity throughout India to the action taken and the reasons for it. In this view the Viceroy had the unanimous support of his Interim Government. It was important that he should also be assured that this policy had the support of His Majesty's Government.

Cat ref: CAB 128/10

Cat ref: PREM 8/541/10

June Plan

The plan to partition was announced in Parliament on 3 June 1947 and on the same day an announcement was made in India. The plan emphasised the necessity for power to be transferred speedily.

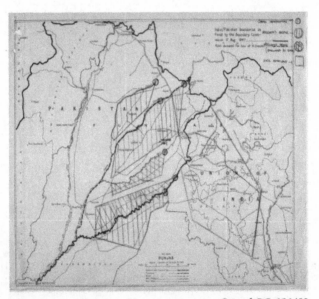

Cat ref: DO 121/69

Independence was granted to two new nations of Pakistan and India on 14 and 15 August respectively. For many millions the reality of Partition only dawned on them after the celebrations had ended. Leaving ancestral lands, people fled – uncertain of their destination on a border that was still very fragile.

Immediate fallout from Partition and the Lord Ismay report

Those charged with providing safe passage and stemming the worst excesses were overwhelmed and heavily compromised. Those witnessing the violence were stunned by its ferocity.

THE INDIAN SITUATION

A PERSONAL NOTE BY LORD ISMAY

SECTION I

1. On my way back to India from England towards the end of last July, I concluded my notes with the following passage:-

> "I was worried when I was in England at the prevalence of
> the idea that everything was over bar the shouting.
> Personally I feel that we are nothing like out of the
> wood yet. There is so much explosive material lying
> about and it remains to see whether it can be prevented
> from going off. I am, for example, extremely worried
> about the Sikhs. They imagine that they are going to
> get a far more favourable boundary than, so far as I
> can judge, the Boundary Commission can possibly award
> them. All possible precautions have been taken by the
> despatch to the areas of potential trouble of a joint
> India-Pakistan force under single command, but even so
> it may be a very unpleasant business. The truth of
> the matter is that both sides are in a panic, and
> people do sillier things when they are frightened than they
> do under the stress of any other emotion."

2. These views were shared by many people. It is therefore a mistake to imagine that the storm which broke out in August, and which is still raging, was unexpected. It must, however, be frankly admitted that neither its character nor its extent were anticipated by anyone in authority, whether in India, Pakistan or England.

3. The last two months have been so chaotic that it would be difficult to find two people who agree as to how the trouble started, why it was not checked, what has actually happened, and what is to be the outcome. While, therefore, I have thought it right to set out in this paper my personal conception of the past, and my estimate of the future, I do not claim that either would receive any general measure

-1-

Cat ref: DO 121/69

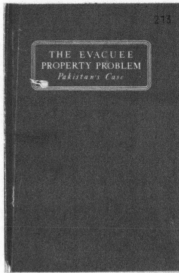

Cat ref: DO 35/2994

Legacy

Historians, like so many others reflecting on this moment in world history, cannot ignore the dark and long shadow cast on the region. In the immediate aftermath of Partition the two new states sought to settle disputes on a whole host of areas, including what each owed the other for those who had been displaced as evacuees.

DISCOVERING RECORDS ONLINE

The National Archives has an online education resource, 'Road to Partition', that is free to access: nationalarchives.gov.uk/education/resources/the-road-to-partition/

Alternatively, you can search and download records online using Discovery, The National Archives' online catalogue: discovery.nationalarchives.gov.uk/

THE NATIONAL ARCHIVES

PARTITION EVENTS

FREE WEBINAR
**RESEARCHING BRITAIN'S
IMPERIAL PAST:
THE COLONIAL OFFICE
RECORDS**
Thu 9 November | 18:00-19:00

TALK AND DOCUMENT DISPLAY
THE PLAN TO PARTITION
Thu 16 November | 18:30-20:00

DISPLAY
PARTITION OF BRITISH INDIA
October 2017-February 2018

To find out more or book
any events, visit:
**nationalarchives.gov.uk
/whatson**

VISITING

The National Archives is the
official archive of the UK
government, and England and
Wales. Open to all, it offers a
range of activities and spaces
to enjoy, as well as our reading
rooms for research.

OPENING HOURS
Monday CLOSED
Tuesday 09:00-19:00
Wednesday 09:00-17:00
Thursday 09:00-19:00
Friday 09:00-17:00
Saturday 09:00-17:00
Sunday CLOSED

The National Archives
Kew
Richmond
Surrey TW9 4DU
Tel: +44 (0) 20 8876 3444
Web: nationalarchives.gov.uk

The Outreach team at The National Archives gratefully acknowledges the work of the historian Yasmin Khan in preparing our Partition programme.

Introduction to *Child of the Divide*

Sarah Ansari

*Royal Holloway, University of London,
and member of the Partition History Project[1]*

*Life goes on and on. Its ends never meet. Neither in the mundane
world of realities, nor in fiction. We drag on drearily in the hope
that someday these ends may meet. And sometimes we have the
illusion that the ends have really joined.[2]*

The opening lines of Bhisham Sahni's short story 'Pali', which
provided the direct inspiration for *Child of the Divide*, capture
splendidly the potent mix of imagination and reality that is the
hallmark of Sudha Bhuchar's dramatic retelling of the Partition
of British India through a child's eyes. For much of the period
since 1947, a collective amnesia has operated when it comes
to reminding ourselves what people living in Pakistan and India
have in common, rather than what separates them. More recently,
however, whether in the form of oral testimonies and traditions,
published biographies, newspaper articles or simply what they
tell their grandchildren, elderly Indians and Pakistanis (and
perhaps also Bangladeshis) who migrated thanks to Partition have
become more willing to reminisce about the homes that they left
behind. As we all appreciate, food together with smells, faded
photographs and half-remembered tunes are all highly evocative
of distant places and earlier times: drawing directly on our most
intimate senses, they resurrect forgotten memories and transport
us back in an instant to worlds that may no longer exist, whether
to our own childhoods or earlier nostalgic moments in our lives.
Among other memories, these aging Pakistanis and Indians still
recall the juiciness of the giant lychees that grew plentifully in
Uttar Pradesh (formerly the United Provinces), or the lushness of

---

[1] Prompted by the seventieth anniversary of Partition in 2017, the
'Partition History Project' was set up to raise understandings of Partition
in UK schools, and, by doing so, to help overcome the negative legacies
dating from 1947 that linger into the present. By bringing together school
teachers, interfaith groups, arts practitioners and academic historians at
Royal Holloway, University of London, its aim was to transform historical
sensitivities and suspicions into something much more positive and less
divisive, with resonance for young people from a range of backgrounds in
the UK today.

[2] First line of Bhisham Sahni's short story 'Pali'.

mangoes cultivated in what was then undivided Punjab, and in the process they fondly savour recollections of their childhoods that were lived in places that are now across the borders drawn up when Independence took place in August 1947.

Seven decades on from the harrowing events of 1947, it is clearly the case that the vast majority of people still alive today who witnessed Partition first-hand did so as children. Most members of this generation of Indians, Pakistanis and Bangladeshis are likely to have been no more than ten years old when South Asia won its freedom from British rule. Like Pali and his friends in *Child of the Divide*, many of them will have been caught up in the turmoil of the time, forced to migrate to a new home or separated from kith and kin for reasons that will have remained a mystery to them until they were much older. These memories, however, may now be fragmentary; moreover, they may well have been influenced by Partition's enduring political legacies that have helped generate and sustain stereotypes alongside hatreds both within South Asia itself and among the South Asian diaspora. Stories of Partition violence, after all, have played a direct part in reinforcing enduring notions that Hindus, Sikhs and Muslims possess sharply-differentiated identities and hence fundamentally opposed interests.

But according to Urvashi Butalia, whose pioneering 1998 study *The Other Side of Silence* was among the first to capture the elusive Partition-related testimonies of ordinary people, and which directly inspired Sudha Bhuchar to write *Child of the Divide*, 'No history of Partition ... so far has had anything to say about children'.[3] The harsh fact is that their experiences have rarely been factored into historical accounts of this momentous event, and this despite the fact that Partition affected the lives of children from all communities hugely both in the short and longer terms. Like women, described by Nehru (India's first Prime Minister) as Partition's 'chief sufferers',[4] children represented 'looted chattels'.[5]

---

[3] Urvashi Butalia, *The Other Side of Silence: Voices from the Partition of India* (New Delhi: Penguin Press, 1998).
[4] *Selected Works of Jawaharlal Nehru*, ed. S. Gopal (2nd series, New Delhi, 1986–1993), vol. 4, p. 196, cited by Andrew J. Major, '"The chief sufferers": Abduction of women during the partition of the Punjab', *South Asia: Journal of South Asian Studies* 18, 1 (1995), pp. 57–72.
[5] Yasmin Khan, *The Great Partition: the Making of India and Pakistan* (New Haven and London: Yale University Press, 2007), p. 128.

Orphaned, lost, abandoned, large numbers of them suffered its trauma first hand, parted for varying lengths of time or perhaps forever from their birth families for one reason or another. Others – such as those born after August 1947 to women 'abducted' by men from other communities – found their legitimacy questioned, and like their mothers they were often sent later to live in whichever of the two new countries was deemed to be the 'right place' for a Muslim or a Hindu or a Sikh. And in a similar fashion to their mothers, who when they were located could be repatriated against their will, children usually had little say in the whereabouts of their future lives.

***

Shortly before midnight on 14/15 August 1947, Jawaharlal Nehru, then leader of the Indian National Congress (the main nationalist organization in British India), rose in India's Constituent Assembly in New Delhi to deliver his famous 'Tryst with Destiny' speech that marked and celebrated the end of two hundred years of British rule in South Asia:

> Long years ago we made a tryst with destiny, and now the time comes when we shall redeem our pledge, not wholly or in full measure, but very substantially. At the stroke of the midnight hour, when the world sleeps, India will awake to life and freedom. A moment comes, which comes but rarely in history, when we step out from the old to the new, when an age ends, and when the soul of a nation, long suppressed, finds utterance.

Earlier that same day, with the last British Viceroy Lord Mountbatten in attendance, leader of the All-India Muslim League Muhammad Ali Jinnah had addressed the newly-created Pakistan Constituent Assembly in Karachi with his own 'Message to the Nation'.

What these two speeches tell us is that the flipside of Independence – long in the making (the Congress had been established as far back as 1885, the League not much later in 1906) – was Partition, the territorial division of British India along ostensibly religious lines to create two separate states in the shape of India and Pakistan (with Pakistan intended as a future home for some though by no means all of British India's Muslims). Britain's withdrawal from its 'Jewel in the Crown' (India was the most important part of its remaining empire by 1947) in practice turned out to be extremely hurried, influenced by the realization by politicians back in London that, with its economy devastated by the Second World War, Britain could not afford to hold on to its over-extended empire. In early 1946 an Act of Parliament had proposed that June 1948 be the deadline for the transfer of power into Indian hands, but the date of independence was later brought forward in early 1947 to August that year by Mountbatten, who had arrived in New Delhi with a mandate to find a speedy way of bringing the Raj (British rule) to its conclusion. By doing this Britain certainly avoided the expensive, protracted war of independence in which other European colonial powers engaged after 1945, but, all the same, the way in which independence took place incurred enormous human cost, linked in large part to the massive population disruptions that Partition triggered.

Until very late in the day, the Congress was still seeking the creation of a unitary and centralized independent India. This objective was challenged by the Muslim League, which – thanks to its 1945–46 electoral successes in provinces with local Muslim majorities such as the Punjab and Bengal – claimed to speak for the subcontinent's Muslim minority (roughly one-fifth of the population in 1947) as a whole. What exactly League leaders wanted, however, has long intrigued historians: did they really want the creation of a separate state for India's Muslims or was Jinnah using this demand as a 'bargaining counter' so as to safeguard the position of Muslims as a religious minority within a future loosely-federated independent India?[6] But either way the political stalemate of the post-Second World War years made compromise unachievable and, with Britain determined to relinquish control over its Indian territories as quickly as conveniently possible, the stage was set for a bloody end of empire.

From March 1947, as uncertainties increased, inter-religious communal violence blazed across northern India, leaving death, destruction and, increasingly, displaced people in its wake. As a Muslim student at Lucknow University in northern India at the time later recalled,

> Nobody [then] thought in terms of migration in those days; the Muslims all thought that everything would remain the same, Punjab

---

[6] Ayesha Jalal, *The Sole Spokesman: Jinnah, the Muslim League and the Demand for Pakistan* (Cambridge: Cambridge University Press, 1994).

would remain Punjab, Sindh would remain Sindh, there won't be any demographic changes – no drastic changes anyway – the Hindus and Sikhs would continue to live in Pakistan ... and we would continue to live in India.[7]

But events proved this particular eye-witness very wrong. Thanks to the deadlock in political negotiations, the 'price' of independence – in effect – became Partition. Up to one million civilians in the end died as local-level violence combined with contagious disease gripped in particular the north-western province of the Punjab, which, like the province of Bengal in the east, was cut in two. Partition accordingly changed the lives of millions on both sides of the hastily drawn-up new borders, which were worked out in just six weeks between June and August 1947 by a commission headed up by British lawyer Cyril Radcliffe, who admitted that he had little knowledge of Indian conditions and relied on out-of-date maps and census materials. Pakistan took the form of a state comprised of two halves: one in the east (formerly East Bengal, now Bangladesh) and the other located 1,700 kilometres away on the western side of the subcontinent, with India in the middle.

The weeks and months straddling 14/15 August 1947 were accompanied by riots, mass casualties and millions of people travelling on foot, in bullock carts and by train to what they hoped would be safer territory. According to a *Daily Mail* correspondent, train station platforms were 'packed with [panic-stricken] Hindu and Sikh refugees waiting despairingly for transport to India', while coming from the other direction 'Muslim refugees from India ... all . . . with an utterly dazed ... air': trains from Delhi to Lahore with enough room for 'a thousand persons at least' arrived at their destination with battered Muslim survivors on board. As headlines in *The Times* of London stated towards the end of September, '4 million on the move in Northern India. Minorities in a state of panic'.[8] This turned out in due course to constitute the largest mass migration that the world has ever seen, with some historians suggesting that the final total may have amounted to as many as 14–16 million uprooted from their homes: according to 1951 censuses of displaced persons, 7,226,000 Muslims went to Pakistan

---

[7] Quoted in Gyanendra Pandey, *Remembering Partition: Violence, Nationalism and History in India* (Cambridge: Cambridge University Press, 2001), p. 26.

[8] Quoted in Pandey, *Remembering Partition*, p. 36.

from India, while 7,249,000 Hindus and Sikhs moved in the other direction. Migration on this scale stunned contemporaries, few of whom had expected to see so many people on the move. All the same, threaded through the undoubtedly traumatic events of 1947 were more positive encounters when people from all communities helped others to survive the brutalities of Partition-related violence, and so buried under the debris of the violence and pain of Partition lies an inspiring if less familiar history of help, humanity and harmony.

Not surprisingly perhaps, the chaotic circumstances that accompanied Partition has made it impossible to pin down the exact figures involved. There are no statistics of the number of children abandoned, abducted, lost, or even adopted, though it often made a difference – as the experience of Sita/Hasina in *Child of the Divide* demonstrates – if the child was a girl or a boy:

> Abducted boys were often used as soldiers against the enemy in 'killing sprees'; girls were often 'sold into prostitution'. Adopted boys were often raised as the family's children; girls were used for 'other services', such as domestic help. Religion, too, was a factor; some claimed Muslims abducted and adopted more Hindu and Sikh boys, believing they were more intelligent, albeit physically weaker, than Muslim boys.[9]

Either way, very little concrete evidence of a child's perspective on Partition has made its way into official records now stored in archives, whether in South Asia or beyond. Instead, it is oral historians who have been at the forefront of finding and piecing together these missing elements of the Partition 'story', and it is on the internet where many of the reconstructed individual life stories can now be found.[10]

***

In *Child of the Divide*, Sudha Bhuchar presents us with the bittersweet tale of a young Hindu boy, Pali, who is adopted by a kindly Muslim couple when he becomes separated from his

---

[9] Paola Bachchetta, 'Reinterrogating Partition Violence: Voices of Women/ Children/Dalits in India's Partition', *Feminist Studies* 26, 3 (Autumn 2000), p. 581.
[10] Examples of online oral archives include: http://www.1947partitionarchive. org/; http://www.andrewwhitehead.net/partition-voices.html; and https:// soundcloud.com/citizensarchive.

parents in the confusion of Partition. Some years later, his birth father returns to what is now Pakistan in order to find and take him 'home', wherever that may be. This raises all sorts of dilemmas for everyone involved: his original parents, his adoptive mother and father, and not least Pali himself. *Child of the Divide*, as already mentioned, is based on a short story, on a piece of fiction. But real life, when we dig a bit deeper, contains similar agonizing episodes when ordinary people – like Pali and his two sets of parents – were forced to confront head-on the painful complications that Partition left in its wake. Take the following incidents that raised similar heart-breaking predicaments which took place in Pakistan in the mid-1950s, just when Pali's own future had to be decided on this particular side of the new dividing line.

Nearly ten years after Partition, in 1956, the issue of the disputed status of children born to 'abducted women' reached the West Pakistan High Court in Lahore. In July that year, one Muhammad Yusuf, living in Rawalpindi (Pakistani Punjab), submitted a writ petition in which he claimed that two children born to an abducted woman who had been living with him since 1948 had been repatriated along with her to India by the authorities, despite the fact that they were bona fide Pakistani citizens and should not be taken away from their father. According to his appeal, Banti (alias Rahmat Jan) had lived with him for around eight years. During this period, she had given birth to a girl (Piari Jan) and a boy (Muhammad Fayyaz), aged six years and two-and-a-half years respectively. In May 1956, all three were 'recovered' by Pakistani officials, and transferred two days later to a non-Muslim transit camp in readiness for their removal to India. In early June, the distraught father submitted his petition to the Divisional Bench. The Court immediately issued a stay order, in theory restraining the authorities from repatriating Piari Jan and Muhammad Fayyaz. Nevertheless, a joint Indo-Pakistan tribunal decided that the mother with her children should be 'returned' to India, and all three were sent across the border to Jullundhur in Indian Punjab later that month. The court then directed lawyers to establish how it would be possible to bring the children back, and the hearing was adjourned in mid-July on the grounds that, until they had actually been retrieved, it would be useless to proceed further with the petition. Banti, it seemed, was unable to decide about the whereabouts of her children's future until she had met her relatives, now in India. There was always the possibility, therefore, that they might be released if those same relatives turned out to be reluctant to accept them along with their mother. But what happened next – unfortunately – is not known.[11]

A second case that came before the same West Pakistan High Court around the same time similarly concerned the status of a child whose parents' relationship was deeply problematic in the eyes of the state. According to contemporary reports, Sardar Abdullah Gill (formerly Arjan Singh), the Sikh headmaster of a school in Moga (Indian Punjab), had married a Muslim woman, Karam Bibi, after apparently rescuing her during the riots of 1947. Karam Bibi, however, was later brought to Pakistan against her will (so it was claimed) by Recovery of Abducted Persons staff in the early 1950s, tasked following agreements between India and Pakistan with tracking down and 'repatriating' such women whether they liked it or not. Arjan Singh then converted to Islam in Delhi, and crossed over into Pakistan with the couple's son, Mushtaq, in order to meet up with his wife. But the couple were arrested in May 1954 and charged with immigration misdemeanours. They, along with their young son (who cannot have been more than six or seven years old by then), were put in prison until the end of their trial, which lasted more than sixteen months. When the couple were convicted, Mushtaq was placed in police custody pending further orders. Following a subsequent appeal, Gill and Karam Bibi were acquitted – and released in September 1955 – but Mushtaq continued for some undetermined reason to be detained by the police. After some time, following the filing of a successful *habeas corpus* petition in July 1956, a judge ordered Mushtaq to be produced before the West Pakistan High Court. A week later, he was finally brought to Lahore and handed over to his much-relieved parents.[12]

Unlike the previous case, we do know what happened to Mushtaq. But in much the same way as the unfinished story of Piari Jan and Muhammad Fayyaz, it highlights the uncertainties that affected how the state and wider society viewed the status of children – like Pali in *Child of the Divide* – whose family circumstances were forever complicated by Partition and its legacies.

---

[11] 'Children born to Abducted Woman', *Pakistan Times*, 12 July 1956, p. 10; *Dawn*, 18 July 1956, p. 1.
[12] *Pakistan Times*, 14 July 1956, p. 10.

Glossary

A salaam walaikum	Peace be with you
Abu/Abba	Father (term used by Muslims)
Acha	Yes
Allah ki kasam	I swear by Allah
Allah Mian Allah	One True God
Al ham dullilah	Praise be to God
Ammi/Amma	Mother (term used by Muslims)
Anna/annas	Item of currency/plural
Atma is Amar	Soul is eternal
Azaan	The call to prayer
Babu	Master
Bacho	Children
Bada aaya	Who do you think you are?
Badmash	Villain/rascal (endearment when about a child)
Bahen	Sister
Baisakhi	Harvest festival in Punjab
Bakwaas	Nonsense
Banda/Bande	Person/people
Bante	Marbles
Baraat	Groom's wedding procession
Beta	Literally 'son' but an endearment for any child
Beta Salaam karo	Child please greet
Bhai/Bhai Sahib	Brother/respected term for brother
Bhagwan	Hindu term for God
Bhajo/Bhago	Run
Budda/Budda baba	Old man
Burra aadmi	Big man
Bus	Enough
Buttameez	Without manners
Chalo	Let's go
Chunri	Long scarf. Same as 'dupatta'
Daal	Lentils
Dada	Paternal grandfather
Dadi	Paternal grandmother
Darpok	Coward
Darvaza Kholo	Open the door
Desh	Country/homeland

Desi Bartan	Local utensils
Dhoti	A long cloth worn by Hindu men as trousers
Diwali	Hindu Festival of Lights when Lord Ram returned from 14 years in exile
Dua (du'a)	Personal prayer or supplication to God
Dupatta	Long scarf, often for covering the head. Same as 'chunri'
Eid	Islamic festival. There are two: one at the end of Ramadan and one at the end of the pilgrimage of Hajj, signifying Abraham's sacrifice
Gajar ka halva	A pudding made from carrots and milk
Gora/Goras	Literally White/the Whites, referring to the English
Gudiya	literally 'doll'; the name of Pali's sister
Hai!/Hai Ram	Oh/oh God – a plantive cry
Hai meri	Oh my!
Han	Yes
Idhar aana	Come here
Inshallah (Insha allah)	God willing
Jaadu ki pudiya	Little packet of magic
Jaldi	Quickly
Janab	Honourable sir
Kafir	Non-believer
Kagaz	Paper/papers
Kalma	The first oath taken by every Muslim; literally 'there is only one God and Mohammed is his Prophet'
Kazi	Judge
Keema	Mincemeat
Khala/Khalas	Aunt (mother's sister/sisters)
Khatai/Khatais	A type of biscuit/biscuits
Kheer	Pudding made from rice and milk
Khuda Hafiz	May God be with you
Kiddan!	How's it going?
Kikli kaleer di	A meaningless rhyme to start the song
Kithe	Where
Kudhi	Girl
Lab pe aati hai dua bankay tamanna meri...	On my lips, my hopes in the form of a prayer – a famous poem/song by the poet Iqbal

La illaha il lalha, Mohammed rasul Allah	Same as 'kalma'; the oath taken by Muslims
Laddoo/laddoos	A type of sweetmeat usually served at big celebrations
Lafanga	Loafer/vagabond
Lathi	Stick
Lori	Lullaby
Maidan	Open ground
Mama kilti	Pali's baby name for quilt
Manj	To clean
Manj the pande	Clean the utensils
Maro isko	Hit him
Mataji	Mother (term used by Hindus)
Maulvi	Muslim clergy
Mohalla	Neighbourhood
Mosque	Place of worship in Islam
Murghi	Chicken
Namaaz	Muslim prayer recited five times a day
Namaste	Hindu greeting with joint palms
Nana	Maternal grandfather
Nani	Maternal grandmother
Pagal Head	Mad Head
Paisa	smallest unit of currency, rather like pence
Pande	Utensils
Pandit	Hindu priest
Paneer	Full fat cheese
Pariah	Outsider
Pitaji	Father (term used by Hindus)
Pithu	A game played with piled-up stones
Pupho/puphos	Aunt/aunts (literally father's sister/sisters)
Purdah	Veil
Rabba	My God
Rakhi	Decorative thread tied by a sister on her brother's wrist to keep him safe
Rehn de	Leave it
Rukko	Stop
Shami kebabs	Kebabs made from mince meat
Shukar al ham dullilah	Thanks be to Allah
Soné	My beautiful
Suna hai	I hear

Taar	Wire/string (of the kite in this instance)
Tarey	Stars
Tava	Flat hot plate pan for cooking, for instance, chappatis
Theeka?	Alright? (colloquial greeting)
Toba Toba	To mean 'Dear, dear God'
Tonga Wallahs	Horse and cart drivers
Tulsi	Basil plant which is holy to Hindus
Tutte Phutte	Broken
Walaikum Salaam (wa'laykum Salaam)	And peace be with you too

Child of the Divide

For
Samar, Sinan, Sana, Zara, Sofia, Ayla, Aisha,
Jaya, Daniyal, Noah, Benjamin and Poppy

Inspired by the short story 'Pali' by Bhisham Sahni

Characters

Pali *(later* **Altaaf***)*
Manohar Lal, *Pali's father*
Kaushalya, *Pali's mother*
Refugee One
Refugee Two
Shakur
Zainab, *Shakur's wife*
Maulvi, *Muslim clergy*
Official
Aisha
Hasina
Buttameez
Pagal Head
Man
Woman

Scene One

Sounds of fireworks and jubilant crowds melt into urgent sound of lorries revving up. Shouts are heard from people along the lines of 'lorries are leaving for the border', 'hurry . . . Jaldi' etc.

Pali*'s house.*

We come up on **Pali**, *a boy of five with his parents,* **Manohar Lal** *and* **Kaushalya**, *in their house. They have a few possessions in bundles and a suitcase, clearly as though they are leaving.* **Kaushalya** *is carrying a baby,* **Gudiya**, *in her arms. The sounds continue.*

Manohar Lal   Chalo Kaushalya. We agreed. No looking back.

Pali   I want to take my marbles from my secret hidey hole!

Manohar Lal   Your mother had to bury her bridal jewellery. Everything will be safe.

Kaushalya   We'll buy you marbles there.

Pali   I don't want to go.

Kaushalya   We have no choice . . .

Pali   But my friends?

Kaushalya   You'll make new friends.

Pali   I want the same friends.

Manohar Lal   One day, God willing, we'll come back home.

Pali   Where are we going?

Manohar Lal   Across the border. India.

Pali   This is India.

Manohar Lal   It was. But not anymore . . .

(Internal voice.)
  How to say to my boy
  The soil he stands on
  No longer welcomes him as a son?

(*To* **Pali**.) Now they've made this into a new country. Pakistan.

Pali   Did God make it?

Manohar Lal   Not God . . .

Pali   Who then?

Kaushalya   So many questions.

Manohar Lal   People . . . the white rulers. And us who don't trust ourselves to live together.

Pali   I didn't see you make it.

A huge firework is let off.

Manohar Lal   It's all right, son. Just the Freedom celebrations.

Pali   Scaring me.

Kaushalya   Adults are jumping out of their skins, let alone children.

Manohar Lal (*internal voice*)
    Fireworks drown
    Screams and cries
    Of people divided.
    'A new dawn', they said
    And carved my country in two.
    Borders and lines
    The price of freedom.
    Hindus to the right,
    Muslims to the left.
    I bundle up my family
    And follow blind.
    I would have liked a say
    In our fate.

We're in the hands of God.

Kaushalya   God has lost his faith today. Where does it leave us?

Pali   If I die will my soul come back?

Manohar Lal   Your soul is everlasting, son. Atma is Amar. No sword can kill it or water drown it. Nor can fire burn it or wind dry it.

Kaushalya   Sh . . . You have your whole life ahead of you.

Pali   When Pitaji's a granddad and you're a grandma, you'll die and me and Gudiya (*meaning the baby*) will be on our own.

Kaushalya   You'll have each other. (*Looking at the thread round* **Pali***'s wrist.*) This rakhi she tied on you . . .

Pali   She didn't tie it . . . she's a baby.

Kaushalya   You know what it means?

Pali   I know, I have to look after her forever . . .

Kaushalya   And her prayers will keep you safe.

Pali   She can't pray.

Urgent voices from outside shouting 'it's not safe for Hindus'.
'Lorries are leaving for the border. Hurry' etc.

Scene Two

Outside near where the lorries are leaving.

Manohar Lal   Come on.

He gathers his family and their few possessions together. **Pali** *tries to rush back as he's forgotten something.*

Pali   My mama kilti. (*His baby word for quilt.*)

Manohar Lal   Leave it.

Kaushalya   He can't sleep without his quilt.

Manohar Lal *reluctantly runs and gets it as a movement section begins whereby the Hindus are scrambling to get on the lorries. There is a great storm of action as people throw luggage on and others get*

disgruntled as they throw it off to make room for more people.
Improvisation of very sparse dialogue. People scramble onto the
lorries and others complain of being squashed. **Kaushalya** *gets on*
with the baby and as **Manohar Lal** *is about to get on he realises that*
Pali *is no longer holding onto his finger. He starts shouting for him*
as the lorry revs up to go.

Refugee One   Get in get in.

Manohar Lal   Pali! Pali!

Refugee Two   Get in. He'll get on another lorry.

Kaushalya   Hai! Hai! Stop the lorry. Pali!

Refugee One   Get on or off.

Refugee Two   You want to look for your child, look. Let
us go!

Kaushalya*'s screams get louder as the lorry moves off.*

Scene Three

Zainab *and* **Shakur***'s house.*

Pali *is asleep in* **Zainab***'s lap wrapped around in his quilt. She is*
holding him quietly.

Shakur   Why so silent Zainab?

Zainab   Too scared to speak.

Shakur (*internal voice*)
   Even in fear
   She looks more beautiful
   Than before.
   Complete.
   His little body
   Clinging to her curves.
   Pariah, yet still
   A perfect fit.

All the Hindus have left their homes. They've gone for good.

Zainab   Maybe we should leave him from where you picked him up. I'm scared we'll be cursed.

Shakur   Others are looting shops, stealing wives. They should be cursed. We are giving a child shelter, Zainab. We will be rewarded.

Zainab   My lap has been empty all these years . . .

Shakur   God works in mysterious ways.

Zainab   He's not ours. How can we keep him?

Shakur   The lorries have gone, Zainab. Allah only knows if his parents are alive.

Zainab   Promise me, Shakur, you looked everywher for them?

Shakur   Allah ki kasam. I was selling my china and pande in Nanak Pura when I realised all the Hindus had left. There was only this boy at the end of the lane, crying for his Pitaji. I took his hand and said, 'Come, we'll find your father!' He took me to the place from where the convoy of lorries had left, but by then even the dust raised by them had long since settled and the place was deserted. It was dark. So I picked him up and brought him home. He was so tired, he fell asleep on my shoulders.

Zainab   Poor thing. Three days he's been crying for his mataji and pitaji.

Shakur   Even if we took him to the police, they can't restore him to his parents.

Zainab   We are God-fearing people. You have done what you can.

She looks at the sleeping **Pali**.

Zainab (*internal voice*)
    I would shut my ears
    To the lullabies
    Of mothers,

Their sweet voices
Mocking my pain.
Dare I hope
To sing him a lori
Of my own?

What's his name?

Shakur   When I asked him he said Pali.

Zainab   These Hindus have such odd names. If I'd had a son, I would have called him Altaaf.

Shakur   Well from today, he is Altaaf. We have found a son and he has found parents.

Pali *wakes up and starts to cry again.*

Zainab   Cry, son. Let the ocean out or you'll drown inside.

She comforts him.

He's so little.

Just then **Aisha**, *a little girl of about six, appears at the doorway. She is unkempt with matted hair but is a complete live wire, older than her years.*

Zainab   How many times I've told you not to creep up on people?

Aisha   Ammi's really depressed today so your clothes aren't ready.

Zainab   Your mother! I told her I needed that suit for Eid. Has she fed you today?

Aisha   She forgot.

Pali *recognises* **Aisha**. **Shakur** *and* **Zainab** *become concerned.*

Pali   Aisha!

Zainab   You know him?

Aisha   He's from my mohalla. (*To* **Pali**.) Ammi said you'd gone to India like all the other Hindus.

Pali I got lost . . . pitaji and mataji are gone . . .

Aisha Wish my ammi would get lost.

Zainab Toba toba. Don't stay that.

Aisha It's true.

Shakur (*to* **Pali**) You can stay here till your pitaji and mataji come for you.

Aisha Zainab mani is nice. She feeds me orange rice.

Pali When will they come?

Shakur Inshallah, soon.

Pali *sees a cat in the courtyard.*

Pali Look, a cat.

Aisha Where?

Pali There. He's jumped off the wall.

Aisha It's chasing the butterfly. Come on, let's run after it.

Zainab No! Stay inside.

Pali Can Aisha stay and play?

Aisha Please!

Shakur Let them play.

Zainab Just for a while but don't tell your ammi about Pali,

Aisha Why?

Zainab Just promise.

Aisha Allah ki kasam.

Zainab I'll bring you two some milk and khatais.

She indicates for **Shakur** *to come aside.*

Zainab If Aisha knows him, he will be recognised by others.

Shakur He's only safe within these four walls.

Zainab *leaves.*

Pali   Why am I a secret?

Aisha   Hindus have to hide or run away.

Pali   Like the butterfly.

Aisha   It's flown away to find a friend, but you have a friend.

Pali   You. And I'm your secret.

Aisha   My ammi says secrets are special.

Pali   My mataji said to never have secrets. To tell her everything.

Aisha   My ammi tells me everything but then she makes me cross my heart and hope to die.

Pali   I hope you don't die.

Aisha   I won't, silly. Can you do a butterfly with your hands?

Pali *copies her, with his quilt still wrapped around him.*

Pali   I like butterflies because they've got nice colours and patterns on them.

Aisha   They're like snails but they've got wings.

Pali   Snails carry their houses but butterflies are born from their houses.

Aisha (*touching his quilt*)   You look like a butterfly wrapped with this. Are these your wings?

Pali   It's my mama kilti. When I was little, I couldn't say 'quilt'. It's from mataji's old sarees.

Zainab *comes back with their snacks.*

Zainab   Here, bacho. Shami kebabs and fresh khatais.

Pali *grabs a kebab hungrily.*

Aisha   You can't eat those. It's meat.

Zainab   It's keema. Eat if you're hungry, beta.

Shakur   Should you have done that?

Zainab   There are worse sins.

Shakur   You will win him through his stomach like you did me.

There is a loud knock on the door.

Zainab   They've come. The people to whom he belongs.

Shakur   Could be anyone.

Another blow at the door. Like a lathi crashing against it.

Maulvi (*off*)   Darvaza kholo! Open the door!

Zainab   Go inside, bacho! Stay quiet.

Pali   I'm scared.

Aisha   I'm not.

Shakur *goes to open the door and* **Zainab** *puts on her veil as she is in purdah in front of men other than her husband. The* **Maulvi** *enters.*

Shakur   Asalaam walaikum, Maulvi sahib.

Maulvi   Walaikum salaam. Suna hai you are harbouring a non-believer in the house, a kafir boy.

Shakur   I have no kafir.

Maulvi   The town's men are ready to raid your place, Shakur bhai, so if you have something to confess . . .

Shakur   Maulvi sahib, I have only given shelter to an orphan boy.

Maulvi   Bring him out to me at once.

Zainab   I have adopted the child, Maulvi sahib. Is it a sin to adopt a child?

Maulvi   In front of whom have you adopted this child? Was there a Kazi? Witness?

Shakur   Allah is our witness.

Maulvi   You don't fear the wrath of Allah, bahen? You give a non-believer a place in your lap?

Zainab   He's just a small boy.

Maulvi   Does he know the kalma?

Shakur   We'll teach him.

Maulvi   Have you had him circumcised?

Silence. Clearly **Shakur** *and* **Zainab** *hadn't thought of that.*

Maulvi   Bring him to the Mosque tomorrow. We'll whisper the azaan in his ear, give him a Muslim name and do the circumcision.

Zainab   We'll bring him, Maulvi sahib. We'll make him our son Altaaf in front of the whole town.

Maulvi   On judgement day Allah will reward you for this. Khuda hafiz.

Shakur/Zainab   Khuda Hafiz.

The **Maulvi** *goes.*

Zainab
   Shukar al ham dullillah
   We don't have to hide
   Like thieves
   With stolen goods.
   We can display our treasure
   For the world to see.

Scene Four

The mosque the next day.

Pali *is at the mosque with* **Shakur** *and the* **Maulvi**. *He still has his little quilt around him. The* **Maulvi** *whispers the azaan in his ear, symbolising that* **Pali** *is being invited into the religion. The* **Maulvi** *then starts to read the kalma.*

Maulvi   La illaha il lalha, Mohammed rasul Allah. Repeat after me. There is only one God and Mohammed is his prophet.

Pali (*holding on to* **Zainab**'s *legs*)   Don't want to.

Zainab   Say what maulvi sahib is asking, soné.

Maulvi   Don't you want God's love?

Pali (*upset*)   God is inside everybody. Pitaji said he's in my blood.

Zainab (*inner voice*)
I too feel
My Allah
As real
As the pulse
On my wrist.
Still we are told
There is them
And there is us

Maulvi   Only if you believe, will God protect you. Once you are a Muslim, nobody will ask who you were before.

Pali   Don't want to say it!

Shakur   You're scaring him, Maulvi sahib.

Maulvi   With the mobs still running wild looking for non-believers, he should be scared.

Shakur   I promise you, I will make him say it. Please, let's finish the other necessaries.

The **Maulvi** *sees the red rakhi thread that is on* **Pali**'s *wrist and with a knife cuts it forcefully.* **Pali** *starts crying.*

Pali   Gudiya!

He carries on crying 'Gudiya!' while holding onto **Zainab**.

Maulvi (*putting a red rumi cap onto the boy's head*)   Al ham
dullilah. Now he is your boy and will have our protection.
Congratulations!

Pali (*inner voice*)
   He cut off the thread, mataji.
   I'm sorry,
   It's not my fault,
   They didn't stop him.
   What will happen
   To Gudiya
   Now the thread is cut
   And I can't protect her?
   I'm sorry mataji,
   It's not my fault.

Scene Five

A refugee camp on the Indian side of the border.

We see **Manohar Lal** *and* **Kaushalya** *with their possessions.*
Kaushalya *places the baby,* **Gudiya,** *on the floor and puts her
dupatta over the face of the child, indicating that the baby has died.
She beats her chest in grief and calls out.*

Kaushalya
   Hai meri Gudiya
   Jaadu ki pudiya!
   My baby doll
   Why am I still here
   And you are gone?
   God should have taken me, Manohar Lal.
   A mother should go
   Before her children
   You should have made him
   Take me.

Manohar Lal   Bus Kaushalya . . . Shh now.

Kaushalya   Don't try to console me, who couldn't save her flesh and blood.

Manohar Lal   None of us were safe from the mob that attacked our lorries.

Kaushalya   Yet we are alive, while my Gudiya was crushed like grain between stones.

Manohar Lal
Kiss her goodbye,
Set her soul free.
She was too good
For this world.
Let her come back
In less troubled times.

Kaushalya   Tell me what sins have I committed to see both my children snatched from me?

Manohar Lal   You have done nothing, Kaushalya. It is the world that has gone mad.

Kaushalya   Where is my Pali? My first baby . . . love of my life, the life in my love. I would shout at him for the smallest thing. Empty anger over spilt daal and dirt. I need to know what has happened to my boy. His strong arms have to be my strength when I am old and grey.

Manohar Lal   I will look for him, I promise. There's an office in Delhi to report lost children. When we reach there, I'll go.

Kaushalya   Where is he? His sister tied a rakhi on him to keep him safe.

Scene Six

Shakur *and* **Zainab**'s *house.*

Pali is in the courtyard dressed in new clothes that clearly show him to be a Muslim boy. He still has his quilt around him. He is looking very festive, which is incongruous with his mood. He is drawing a

picture in the dirt with a stick. It is his mum and dad and a baby.
Zainab *enters wearing a bright suit and carrying a tray of laddoos.*
She goes and offers one to **Pali**. *He shrugs and refuses.*

Zainab   Do you know why we had a party?

Pali *shakes his head.*

Zainab   For you. To welcome you as Altaaf, our son.

Pali   My name is Pali.

Zainab   It's not safe for you to be Pali anymore. Do you
understand that, soné?

Pali *shakes his head, clearly not understanding.* *Silence as* **Zainab**
notices the drawing **Pali** *has made.*

Zainab   Is this your pitaji and mataji?

Pali *nods.*

Zainab   And the baby?

Pali   Gudiya. Mataji grew her in her tummy. Then she
came out and cried so much, I couldn't sleep.

Zainab   I know I didn't grow you from my flesh, but I want
more than anything in the world to give you a mother's love.

Pali   You're not my mum.

Zainab   You know I prayed and prayed and asked dua
from Allah to make me a mother. Twice he answered my
prayers and both times it was not to be. Then he sent you
to me.

Palii (*as he wraps himself around his mama kilti and starts crying*)
I want my mataji!

Zainab   Cry, soné . . . let the ocean out.

Pali   It's a river.

Zainab   And one day it will only be a puddle. Shall we make
a paper boat and float the sadness away?

Pali   My soul hurts.

Zainab *holds him tight. He lets her. She starts to sing a lullaby as she makes a paper boat.*

Zainab (*singing*)
   Titli thi ik titli thi,
   Idhar udhar udti titli thi.
   Upar pankha chale,
   Niche sona soye.
   Ma uski moti,
   Khaye double roti.
   Titli thi, ik titli thi.

   (*English translation as alternative to use.*)

   [Once there was a butterfly
   Here and there it fluttered by.
   Up above the ceiling fan whirred,
   Down below the little boy snored.
   His mother was fat.
   From eating too much bread.
   Once there was a butterfly.
   Here and there it fluttered by.]

Scene Seven

Office in Delhi.

Manohar Lal *and* **Kaushalya** *are filing the case for* **Pali** *being missing.*

Official (*as he is writing on the form*)   Yashpal, aged five, known as Pali. Why people give their sons stupid nicknames like Pali? Palis, Rajus and Guddus are two a paisa. Makes our job harder than looking for a speck of dirt in a sack of chappati flour. My father had the good sense to nickname me Bhundal . . . I hated it as a child . . .

Manohar Lal *and* **Kaushalya** *are bemused by his ramblings.*

Official   From 'Bhondu', meaning Simpleton. Or a harsh translation may be 'without anything (*Tapping his head.*) up here'. I used to get teased by bullies but I'm having the last laugh. Here I am, an official in this new Indian government serving the very first Prime Minister, Jawaharlal Nehru, and where are they? Not bad for a simpleton. So, for example, if I was to get abducted or lost, you can be sure you will be looking for only one Bhundal who fits the bill. So where were we? Pali . . . son of?

Manohar Lal   Manohar Lal and Kaushalya Rani.

Official   Naranag Mandi, Shekhupura district. Any distinguishing features?

Kaushalya (*inner voice*)
His grandfather's eyes,
An angel's smile,
Tousled hair
No comb could tame.
His eyes twinkle
And cheeks dimple,
When he smiles
his monkey smile.

Official   Speak up, I'm a busy man. What shall I fill in here?

Manohar Lal   Bhai sahib, he is an ordinary boy. Only to us he is special. I have a photograph.

Official   Give me and I will file the case.

Manohar Lal   When will you start looking for him?

Official   When the borders reopen, enquiries can begin but I don't hold out hope.

Manohar Lal   I can't tell my wife there is no hope.

Official   Bhai sahib, you are young. Don't waste your time here. Go home and make more babies.

He sees **Manohar Lal**'s *reaction.*

Official   Or embrace another's child. The refugee camps are full of unclaimed children; lost and littered like fallen leaves.

Manohar Lal   I have a boy.

Official   He is gone. Accept it.

Manohar Lal   I will never accept it.

There is a physical vignette here where **Manohar Lal** *is searching and doors are shutting in his face. There is sparse dialogue and possible repetition of the following ending in his utter despair and inner cry.*

Manohar Lal   Have you seen my Pali?

Voice   He's gone. Accept it.

Manohar Lal   We lost him before the troubles.

Voice   Start a new life. Don't look back.

Manohar Lal   Has he been spotted?

Voice   Thousands like him, washed away by the waves of hatred.

Manohar Lal   Has he been seen?

Voice   Who looks at another? Everyone is lost in their own turmoil. Go home. Accept it.

Manohar Lal   I can't. I won't.

(*Inner voice.*)
   If he was dead
   Only then
   Can I accept.
   Shed silent tears
   Like for my baby girl.
   But he is across the border.
   I know he is.
   A few miles between,
   The same stars
   Shine on him.

Scene Eight

Across the border in Pakistan. Wasteland outside the refugee camp.

Four years have passed since **Pali** *disappeared.* **Aisha** *and* **Sita/
Hasina** *come running on. They sing as they skip.* **Aisha** *has
subverted the words of a rhyme. They drag* **Pali** *to join them.*

Song

> Kikli kaleer di
> The turban of my brother.
> Duppatta of my bhabi
> But she loves another.
> She sparkles and she sways,
> She whispers and she sighs,
> Her love is her life,
> But she has her ties.
> My brother will come
> Bringing garlands and flowers
> We'll dance and we'll sing
> But my bhabi's heart cowers.

Hasina *breaks off.*

Hasina   You've changed the words, Aish.

Aisha   My mum taught me. She had a secret love.

Pali   How do you know?

Aisha   Just do . . . She kisses old letters and covers me in
sadness.

Hasina   My ammi had to run away from home to marry
my abu.

Pali   Why?

Aisha   Was that in India where you lived?

Hasina   Yeah.

She realises she's said too much.

Aisha   My ammi says marriage is a curse, but I love weddings. Dancin' in the baraat . . .

Hasina   The groom on a white horse, his face a mystery behind garlands of jasmine . . .

Pali   Cos he's ugly as sin.

Aisha   Oy!

Pali   Marriage is for girls.

Aisha   Yeah, but they like marry boys?

Pali   I'm never getting married.

Aisha   I am. To a man with a scooter and a moustache, which tickles when he kisses my belly button.

Hasina   Aisha!

Pali   Yuck!

Hasina   Have you ever kissed a girl?

Pali   No way.

Buttameez *and* **Pagal Head**, *two older Muslim boys, run on rolling a bicycle wheel with a stick.* **Pagal Head** *is clearly a tougher, leader of the pack type.* **Pali** *and the girls clearly recognise* **Buttameez**.

Buttameez   Theeka Altaaf?

Pali   All right Buttameez!

Pagal Head   You kudhi man? Playing with the girls?

Pali   They're my friends.

Pagal Head   What's that you got around you? (*Pulling* **Pali**'s *quilt*.) Dupatta. Hey, smell this, Buttameez.

Buttameez   I know. It's minging but he won't wash it.

Pagal Head   Why don't you paint your lips red?

Buttameez   Rehn de, Pagal Head.

Pali What kind of name is that?

Making a circle with his finger on the side of his head to indicate that **Pagal Head** *is mad.*

Pali Pagal Head!

Pagal Head *gives him an evil look.*

Pali Just scratching!

Pagal Head It's cos I go mad if anyone mess with my head.

Hasina We're not scared of you.

Pagal Head I know you, Cinderella shoes.

Hasina Hasina.

Pagal Head (*looking at* **Hasina**'s *faded embroidered shoes*) You that refugee kudhi that manj the pande and sweep the houses?

Hasina I'm not refugee.

Pagal Head How comes you live on the camp for Indian refugees? You gotta mum and dad?

Hasina None of your business.

Buttameez What's wrong with the camp, eh, dude?

Pagal Head You tell me. You ran away.

Buttameez That's cos they tried to get me adopted.

Hasina Me too. Except people only want boys so I'm safe.

Buttameez Don't want a new family.

Hasina My ammi will come and get me from India.

Pagal Head You Muslim girl. You live in Pakistan now. You can't go back to India.

Buttameez Wanna play bante?

Pali Yeah all right.

Aisha I'll challenge you.

Pagal Head I only play for high stakes. Winner takes all.

Aisha You're on.

Buttameez Teams?

Pagal Head You and me take on . . .?

Pali Altaaf.

Pagal Head Altaaf and the kudhis against Pagal Head and Buttameez.

Pali You're on.

Buttameez I'm like the unbeatable champion . . .

Aisha Champion from where? India. Well this is Pakistan and we'll see who's champion.

Pali Five marbles each team.

He makes a circle and each team puts five marbles into it. **Pagal Head** *inspects the marbles.*

Pagal Head New ones. Don't want no tutte phutte. The girls' team can go first.

Aisha *crouches down and bending her finger back aims at the circle. She knocks a marble out of the circle and jubilantly swipes all the marbles.*

Aisha Victory screech!

Her team screech together.

Buttameez Beginner's luck.

Pagal Head Double or quits!

Aisha *puts all her marbles into the circle and the other team add ten marbles to the pile.*

Aisha Winner goes first.

Pagal Head Different player though.

Hasina *aims and misses.* **Buttameez** *aims and hits two marbles.*

Pali   Foul! He touched two bante!

Pagal Head   Kithe foul? It's not foul.

Aisha   Put them back.

Pagal Head   You gonna make me?

Buttameez   Put them back Pagal Head. I'll have my go again.

Pagal Head   No. I'm referee and I say we win.

Pali   You can't be referee. You didn't see.

Pagal Head   He's calling me liar.

Buttameez   Rehn de.

Aisha   You're just a bully.

Pagal Head (*sweeping aside the marbles*)   We win. In your face! You're a disgrace! (*To* **Buttameez**.) Chal. Let's go.

Buttameez *and* **Pagal Head** *leave.*

Hasina   Let's follow them. I know where he hides his stash.

Pali   How do you know?

Hasina   I sweep his house. He has a hidey-hole in the back.

Aisha   Come on. Let's get what's ours.

They follow **Pagal Head** *to his house.* **Pali** *has a huge déjà vu moment. He is standing outside his old house. The girls don't notice at first.*

Hasina   Behind the house. He's dug a hole.

Aisha *realises what has happened.*

Pali   This is my house! That's my hidey hole!

Hasina   How can it be your house?

Pali   Why didn't you tell me, Aish? Why didn't you tell me that someone took it?

Aisha   I'm the queen of secrets. Didn't want you to get upset.

Hasina   Upset about what?

Aisha   He used to live here.

Pali   Pitaji said it was as old as history.

Aisha   Pagal Head has seen us!

Pagal Head *and* **Buttameez** *come out.*

Pagal Head   What do you want?

Pali   This is my house. My granddad and great granddad built it.

Aisha   Don't, Altaaf.

Pagal Head   Says who?

Pali   Here my mataji prayed to the tulsi every day. Why is it burnt?

Pagal Head   Who prays to a stupid tree?

Pali   And here I carved my name on the door (*Spelling his name phonetically.*) P . . . A . . . L . . . EE.

Aisha   Oh no!

Pagal Head   I thought your name was Altaaf?

Aisha   Let's go.

Pagal Head   You a Hindu darpok! Why you didn't bhajo all the way to India like the others?

Pali   I'm not scared of you . . . mad head!

Pagal Head   My dad's a burra aadmi. He can make people like you disappear. Kaput! And when you die, you can come back as a fish or something. I can put masala on you and fry you on the tava and eat you.

Pali   You can't just take my house.

Pagal Head   In my food chain, there's like me at the top, no, maybe my ammi and abu, then me, then my dadi, dada, nani, nana, puphos, khalas and cousins, then Muslims from India like Buttameez and you, kudhi, then all the animals and birds and right at the bottom is Hindus like you. This is my dad's house now. Pakistan Zindabad!

Pali *goes to hit* **Pagal Head** *and a fight ensues.*

Aisha/Hasina   Stop it.

Pagal Head   Oy, Buttameez. Maro isko!

Buttameez *joins the blows enthusiastically, displaying an uncharacteristic venom as the girls try to stop the fight.*

Scene Nine

A little while later. **Pali** *is with* **Aisha** *and* **Hasina** *in the Maidan.*

Pali *comforts himself with his quilt.* **Hasina** *wipes his bruises.*

Hasina   I didn't know you was Hindu.

Aisha   He's not. Maulvi sahib made him Muslim.

Pali   Pitaji said people are people, but he lied.

Hasina   Some people are just bad.

Aisha   Like that Pagal Head.

Hasina   And Buttameez. I thought he was our friend.

Aisha   We'll get them.

Pali   They're bigger than us.

Aisha   We'll tell Maulvi sahib and your ammi and abu.

Pali   They're not my mum and dad. My real mum and dad lost me.

Hasina   Maybe they're looking for you.

Pali   I wish I was a baby then they could have carried me like they did Gudiya.

Hasina   Why don't you think about them? If you think about someone really really hard, then they think about you at the same time.

Aisha   That's stupid.

Hasina   It's true. My ammi said.

Pali   I'm scared I'll forget my mataji. (*Burying his head in his quilt.*) But I remember her smell.

Hasina   I think about my ammi all the time and I know she thinks about me.

Aisha   So why doesn't she come and get you?

Hasina   She thinks I'm safe with my uncle.

Pali   So why are you in the refugee camp?

Hasina   Can I tell you a secret?

Aisha   Not another secret? My heart's gonna burst.

Pali   Allah ki kasam, we won't tell.

Hasina   I'm half-half so I got two names. Hasina, cos my abu said I was his beautiful princess, and Sita, which was my secret with my mama.

Pali   Sita? Hindu name like Pali?

Aisha   Lord Ram's wife. We studied it at school. Before all the Hindus left. Now we're not supposed to know. She was kidnapped by that Raavan, isn't it?

Hasina   Sita stayed pure, but like no one believed her and in the end, she asked Mother Earth to take her back.

Pali   I thought Ram and Sita had a happy ending.

Hasina   Mama said Sita was too good for this world. But I'm bad. My uncle said that my abu died because of me.

Pali   S'not true.

Hasina   Hindus killed him cos he married a Hindu and they don't like that. Bloods shouldn't mix. But mine is.

Pali   If you cut do you bleed different colours?

Aisha   Don't be stupid.

Hasina   Because of my Muslim blood, my mama sent me with my Uncle to be safe here in Pakistan. Because of my Hindu blood, my uncle left me by the side of the road. Sitting on a stone . . . alone. He said he couldn't love me because in my face he could see the Hindus that killed his brother. I loved my abba . . . Allah ki kasam . . . He made me pretty things and (*Looking at her battered shoes.*) decorated my shoes with tarey and sequins. A soft lady found me. She took my hand and brought me to the camp across the border. I came with other lost children like Buttameez.

Pali   I never knew that.

Hasina   You're lucky your new mum loves you. She's always calling you in to eat a sweet rusk or khatai.

Pali   It's like she doesn't want me to be hungry. But sometimes her treats stick in my throat and I'm still hungry. I think about my real mum and dad. Why did they lose me?

Aisha   Wish I could take my ammi to the mum swap shop.

Hasina   You don't mean it.

Aisha   I do. I always have to hug and kiss her to cheer her up. It frightens me. When she's angry, I'm calm; when she's upset, I'm cheerful; when she's silly, I'm silly. She plays tickle monster and we laugh and laugh till we cry. Then she can't stop. She even cries on my birthday and Eid. When she's sad, I hate her.

Hasina   My amma will come and get me.

Pali   How do you know?

Hasina   I post her a letter every day.

Buttameez *approaches the trio tentatively.*

Pali   Thought you was my friend.

Buttameez   You didn't tell me you was Hindu.

Aisha   And you didn't tell us you was evil?

Buttameez   Don't you know Hindus hate us?

Hasina   Who says?

Buttameez (*to* **Pali**, *not really hearing* **Hasina**)   I wanna know why you hate us.

Pali   I hate you cos you hit me.

Buttameez   I hit you cos you hate me.

Pali   I don't.

Buttameez   You do. You Hindus told us to leave India.

Pali   And you Muslims told us to leave Pakistan.

Buttameez   I didn't. I wasn't even here.

Pali   And I didn't. I wasn't even there.

Buttameez   I didn't want to leave.

Pali   Nor did I, but I wish I had now.

Buttameez   I just wanted to play bante with my friends.

Pali   Me too.

Buttameez
    But they looked at me,
    And turned away.
    Their eyes
    Pure enemy.

Pali   I didn't turn away from you. You hit me.

Aisha   Just cos that Pagal Head told you to.

Hasina   You should think for yourself, not just follow bullies.

Buttameez (*meaning* **Pali**)   He made me mental. Never seen a Hindu since we walked all the way here from India to get away from them.

Hasina   Yes you have.

Buttameez   Haven't.

Hasina   You've seen me.

Buttameez   You're not one of them.

Hasina   Half of me is them.

Buttameez   Why didn't you say?

Hasina   Didn't want your hate like my uncle's.

Buttameez   Why should I hate you?

Hasina   You'd look at my face and see the Hindus that killed your family.

Buttameez   You're my best friend. Only one from my desh.

Hasina   And Pali . . . Altaaf is my friend.

It sinks in to **Buttameez**.

Buttameez (*to* **Pali**)   Sorry dude.

Pali   Yeah. Me too.

Aisha   What happened to your family?

Buttameez   Nothing.

Pali   If you don't tell, you might forget.

Buttameez   I want to forget but it won't let me.

Aisha   Tell us then.

Buttameez   No!

Hasina   Leave him.

Pali   Come on, let's play tag. Bhago, I'm it.

He hops on one leg and chases the others exuberantly.

Scene Ten

A few months later. India.

Kaushalya *is cleaning as* **Manohar Lal** *bursts in with huge brown packets.*

Manohar Lal   Kaushalya, I'm home!

Kaushalya *barely looks at him and carries on.*

Kaushalya   You're in the way, I'm trying to clean.

Manohar Lal   Leave it. Come, let's go to the Maidan and fly kites.

Kaushalya   The hinge on the door is rusty.

Manohar Lal   I'll fix it later.

Kaushalya   And the walls haven't been whitewashed for two years.

Manohar Lal (*inner voice*)
   She hears, but won't listen.
   She cleans, she cooks,
   And never sits.
   She looks, but her eyes never meet mine.
   Her ruby red lips, grey and pale,
   Never break into a smile.
   The hands that held mine
   Out of reach.
   Her body turned away,
   Out of touch.

(*To* **Kaushalya**.)   Did you hear me, Kaushalya?

He takes huge kites out of the bag.

Kaushalya   Why are you back early? You should be at work.

Manohar Lal   Come on. I challenge you to break my taar.

Kaushalya   Are you out of your mind?

Manohar Lal   Please. Don't say no, Kaushalya. Not today.

Kaushalya   You want the whole world to gloat at my sorrow?

Manohar Lal   You want to stay in these four walls forever?

Kaushalya   I need to finish what I'm doing.

Manohar Lal   You do when nothing needs doing.

Kaushalya   And what would you like me to do? Play like a child when I don't have my child?

Manohar Lal   Do you know what day it is?

Kaushalya   He will be ten. Lost to us for nearly half his life.

Manohar Lal *sits down, deflated.*

Manohar Lal   If we saw him in the street, would we even recognise him?

Kaushalya   Are you asking me to forget?

Manohar Lal   We could have another child.

Kaushalya   Never.

Manohar Lal   If you would only let me comfort you.

Kaushalya   How can you know my pain?

Manohar Lal   I miss him too, you know.

Kaushalya   How could you let his fingers slip through your hand?

Manohar Lal   Not a day goes past when I don't ask myself that.

Kaushalya   You carried a suitcase, when you should have carried our boy. The suitcase is safe but where is my boy?

(Internal voice.)
    Too late.
    I can't swallow them back.
    The words I kept
    Under lock and key,

Poisoning me inside,
They've escaped
From my lips.

Manohar Lal (*internal voice*)
I ask myself
Again and again
How could I let go
Of the little hand
That held mine
So tightly?
I felt his grip
Long after
His fingers had slipped.
In the blink of an eye
He disappeared
From sight.
Rabba take me back
To the place where he was lost,
To the end of the lane
Where in my dream
He still awaits me.

An interval can be put here if deemed appropriate.

Scene Eleven

Two years later. Streets around the town in Pakistan.

Pali *is out peddling china, etc. with* **Shakur**. *They both have a basket over their heads as they cry out. They could use the audience to sell to.*

Pali   Pande! China!

Shakur   English China! Desi bartan!

Pali   Tea set, dinner set! Cup and saucers!

Shakur   Lovely designs. Buy them for your daughters!

Pali   Their mother-in-laws will be impressed!

Shakur   And forget to chide them about their sense of dress!

Pali   They can serve tea like English memsahibs. Milk in first! . . . One lump or two?

Shakur (*showing one of the cups*)   Moonlight Rose, all in blue!

Pali (*showing another pattern*)   Lavender rose for a love that remains true!

Shakur *is very impressed with* **Pali***'s improvisation.*

Shakur   Look at you! Not a hair on your chin and you're peddling romance to my punters.

Pali   People want to be promised more than a cup of tea, abu.

Shakur   Listen to you . . . You imp! The way you shifted those soup bowls to old Mrs Khan! What did you promise her? A kiss?

Pali   No. I said to her, 'So what if you don't serve soup like the English? Use them for kheer or gajar ka halva. The silver paper on the sweets will shine like the silver pattern on the bowls'.

Shakur   With me her handkerchief remains tightly knotted in her bosom. Yet for you she parted with a healthy sum.

Pali   Can we put it towards our shop fund?

Shakur   Yes. 'Shakur Ahmed and son', or the rate you're going it should say 'Altaaf Ahmed and father'.

Pali   No, abu. You came before me.

Shakur   What a respectful boy. Your ammi will soon be looking for a bride for you.

Pali   I'll find my own.

Shakur   Acha? Forward in love too?

Pali   Can I ask you something abu?

Shakur   Of course.

Pali   How do you know when you love someone?

Shakur   You mean, like a girl?

Pali   Like ammi?

Shakur (*inner voice*)
In a sea of faces
She glowed
Just for me.
Her deep blue chunri
Glittering like stars,
The sun
In my courtyard.

Your ammi crept into my life and then she took over
my heart.

Pali   How do you know it's love?

Shakur   You know because your heart races, you feel the
breeze with every pore of your skin and you're more alive
than you ever will be.

Pali   How do we know we're alive? How do you know we
even exist?

Shakur   Badmash! I'm a salesman, not a philosopher.

Pinching him.

I pinch you . . .

Pali   Ouch!

Shakur   You're alive.

They start to walk off and come across **Manohar Lal**.

Manohar Lal   Excuse me, Janab. Could you direct me to
Naranag Mandi?

Pali *stares at* **Manohar Lal**. *Seeing someone in Hindu attire is unusual.*

Shakur   Han.

Before **Shakur** *can speak,* **Pali** *dives in.*

Pali   You just carry on straight and then left at Zaman tailors.

Manohar Lal   What used to be Satish tailors?

Shakur   Yes. You are from around here?

Manohar Lal   Before Partition. I lived here.

Shakur   Then you are a son of this soil. Welcome!

Manohar Lal   Thank you.

Manohar Lal *leaves.* **Shakur** *is concerned.*

Pali   Is he from India?

Shakur   Many Hindus are coming. To see their old homes maybe.

Shakur (*inner voice*)
  The borders reopen.
  Neighbours return
  To pick up the threads
  Of a life
  Left behind.
  What will I say
  If he asks again
  Questions
  Long answered
  Of blood and belonging.

Sound of the Muezzin's call to prayer. **Pali** *assuages* **Shakur**'s *fears as he sings nonchalantly.*

Pali
  Get up you pious Muslims,
  Come for namaaz.
  Judgement day is nigh

When the earth will be no more.
Mountains will turn to dust,
Questions will need answers
About your words and deeds.
Take heed. Take heed.
Oh Muslims awaken,
Come for your namaaz!

Shakur   Come on now. Your ammi will be waiting.

Scene Twelve

A little while later.

Pali *and* **Hasina** *are sat on the branch of a tree sucking mangoes, the juice running all over their faces.*

Pali (*looking at* **Hasina**)   Your face is orange and sticky.

Hasina   So is yours.

Pali *wipes it with the side of his fading quilt.*

Hasina   You still carry that?

Pali   You still have your Cinderella shoes.

Hasina   Don't fit me anymore.

Pali   Some boys gotta cummerbund, I got this.

Silence.

Can you feel the breeze with every pore of your skin?

Hasina   It's windy.

Pali   Yeah, but is your heart thumpin'? Do you feel really alive?

Hasina   Is it a trick question?

Pali   No, just asking.

Hasina   I like you if that's what you're asking.

Pali *gets embarrassed.*

Pali   No.

Hasina   I got something to tell you.

Pali   What?

Hasina   The soft lady's getting me adopted.

Pali   Buttameez hasn't got adopted.

Hasina   Yeah but he lives wild. Girls can't do that.

Pali   Where you going?

Hasina   This old budda came and chose me.

Pali   How old is he?

Hasina   I don't know . . . forty-five maybe. He's got sweaty hands and he talks in poetry.

Pali   What did he say?

Hasina   His wife died so he wants me to look after him and his children.

Pali   Like a servant.

Hasina   Like a daughter, he said.

Pali   Say no.

Hasina   I can't. The soft lady said all the other refugee children have got homes now so I can't be fussy.

Pali   What about your mum in India?

Hasina   I send her letters every day but maybe she's not coming.

Pali   I won't let you go. I'll talk to Ammi and Abu.

Scene Thirteen

A little while later. **Pali**'s *house. Pakistan.*

Pali   Why can't Hasina come and live with us?

Shakur   She's not our responsibility.

Pali   But she's my friend.

Shakur   I can't take in your strays and waifs.

Pali   Just her.

Zainab   You are enough for us, beta.

Pali   But you're not enough for me!

Shakur   Altaaf!

Pali   You don't care that she's gonna be a servant to a budda baba?

Shakur   I'm sure that he will look after her.

Pali   You don't know. You don't know anything about him.

Zainab   You will not speak to your abu like that.

Pali   You don't care what happens to my special friend.

Shakur   You can still see her.

Pali   She won't be able to come out and play.

Zainab   Girls at a certain age can't come out and play anyway. You have to play with boys now.

Pali   Then I'll marry her.

Shakur   What's got into him?

Zainab   You're too young to know what you want.

Pali   You can't read my mind.

Shakur   Watch your tongue! Hanging around with those vagabonds and lafangas, you're getting led astray.

Pali   I love Hasina.

Zainab   It's a crush. You could never marry someone like her.

Pali   Why not?

Zainab   She's a refugee. Without family. Without roots.

Pali   You don't know anything about her.

Shakur   And you're the expert?

Zainab   You can't judge the fruit if you don't know what tree it came from.

Pali   I do know. She's from Delhi, India. Her father was Zafar, a tailor. Her mother was Kamla, a teacher's daughter . . .

Shakur   A Hindu . . .

Pali   So was I a Hindu. You didn't care which tree I came from.

Zainab   You're our boy now. That's all that matters.

Pali   And Hasina's my friend. That's all that matters.

Shakur   Trust us to choose what's best for you.

Pali   You said Allah mian says to extend a hand of friendship to everyone but you hate my friends.

Zainab   Friends are not family.

Pali (*running off*)   You are not my family.

Zainab   Beta!

Shakur   Leave him.

Scene Fourteen

A little while later. In the open Maidan.

Buttameez and **Aisha** *run on and alternately pile up five stones as if in the middle of a game of Pithu. When the pile is made, they both shout out.*

Buttameez/Aisha   Pithu!

Pali and **Hasina** *come on.* **Pali** *is aiming a ball at* **Aisha** *to get her out but she has finished the pile before he can hit her.*

Aisha Our turn again.

Buttameez I'll break.

Pali *throws the ball to* **Buttameez** *who hits the stones and breaks them.* **Aisha** *runs to get the ball and aims at* **Hasina** *to try to get her legs. She misses and* **Pagal Head** *catches the ball as he comes on. They all stop in their tracks.*

Hasina You can't play with us.

Pagal Head (*to* **Hasina**) Kiddan! Cucumba cool kudhi!

Pali Leave her alone.

Pagal Head You wanna teach your munda some manners.

Pali Like your manners, you mean.

Pagal Head (*to* **Hasina**) You better be friendly kudhi cos your boyfriend going back to his desh innit? Then you gonna have to be nice to me . . .

Aisha You talking bakwaas.

Pagal Head Allah ki kasam. I come to give you the news. But if you don't wanna know . . .?

Buttameez You got something to say. Spill it out.

Pagal Head Some weirdo babu coming to get you man.

Pali How do you know?

Pagal Head Came to our house innit. My abu ready to kill him if he wants the house back but he just askin' after you.

Pali I don't believe you.

Pagal Head Better believe it. He's got the kagaz, papers proving he's your dad. Take you back to Junglistan with him.

Pali How does he know where I am?

Pagal Head *flashes a smile.* **Pali** *understands that he has told him.*

Buttameez   You told him?

Pagal Head   Just bein' a good citizen.

Buttameez   You shouldn't've done that.

With a stick, **Pagal Head** *manages to whip off* **Pali**'s *quilt.*

Pagal Head   You won't need your minging dupatta.

Pali   Give it back.

Pagal Head   Smell it! His bib. His ma's perfume. Stinks of tutti.

Pali   I'll smash your head in.

Pagal Head   Try it.

Pagal Head *runs off with the quilt. The others follow him and try to stop him.*

Needs a wash. I'm gonna throw it in the river.

Pali   Leave it.

It is too late. **Pagal Head** *has thrown the quilt in the river.* **Buttameez** *grabs him by the collar.*

Buttameez   You gonna fetch that back or I'll kill you.

Pagal Head   You're jokin'?

Buttameez   Try me.

Pagal Head   What are you? Hindu lover? You wanna be my banda . . . I look after you.

Buttameez   I'm my own banda.

Pagal Head   You on your own then.

Buttameez   Get it out.

Buttameez *pushes him by the river and* **Pagal Head** *falls in.*

Pagal Head   I can't swim . . . Help me! . . . Help me . . .

Aisha   Let him drown.

Hasina   We can't do that. Help him!

Pali *rushes in and helps him. They get him out.* **Pagal Head** *is clearly traumatised.*

Aisha   Coward! Calling others darpok!

Pagal Head *is crying, holding onto* **Pali**.

Pali   You're alive. What you crying for?

Pagal Head   I thought I was gonna die like all the others.

Buttameez   What others?

Pagal Head   I saw them, the bodies floatin' in the water . . . the river red with blood . . .

Buttameez   There's no bodies.

Pagal Head   The river is full of bodies. Some running as if they could run on water and escape . . .

Pali   What are you talking about?

Pagal Head   The men and my abu chasin the Hindus . . . the shoutin' and screamin' . . . the men just killing them and throwin' the bodies in the water . . . I never killed anyone I promise . . . I never touched no one . . .

Hasina   It's okay.

Pagal Head   I see the black eyes of a boy looking at me. I wasn't gonna do nothing . . . Allah ki kasam. But he too scared and jump in the water hisself. He can't swim . . . I see him sinking . . . just like a stone . . . sinking to the bottom of the water.

The kids comfort **Pagal Head** *by their presence, not necessarily being able to reach out to him fully.*

Scene Fifteen

Pali's *house, Pakistan.*

There is a loud knock at the door. **Zainab** *in her purdah comes on.*

Zainab   Who is it?

Manohar Lal (*from off*)   My name is Manohar Lal. I am from Hindustan. I need to speak to Mr Shakur Ahmed.

Zainab   Shakur, Shakur, a man has come from Hindustan.

Shakur   Stay inside with Altaaf. Let me talk to him.

Shakur *lets* **Manohar Lal** *in*.

Manohar Lal   Asalaam walaikum Shakur Sahib.

Shakur   Namaste.

Manohar Lal   We met in the street with the boy . . .

Shakur   My son. Altaaf.

Manohar Lal   He gave me directions. I didn't know . . .

Shakur   Please sit.

Manohar Lal *sits down awkwardly*.

Shakur   You have come from far?

Manohar Lal   Delhi.

Shakur   All the way from there. Staying long?

Manohar Lal   As long as it takes.

Shakur   What is your purpose here?

Manohar Lal   I have come for my boy. We lost him when we left this place.

Zainab (*inner voice*)
   This is it
   The long dreaded
   Knock at the door
   But I won't
   Let him go.

Shakur   Hundreds of children got lost in that time.

Manohar Lal   But it is my boy that you gave refuge to and I want to thank you.

Shakur   You can't prove Altaaf is your boy.

Manohar Lal   It has been proven. The authorities have traced him and assured me that he has been living here as your adopted son.

Shakur   He was alone. We looked and waited but no-one came to claim him.

Manohar Lal   How could we come during the troubles?

Shakur   Seven years we have looked after him as our own.

Manohar Lal   I'm grateful, but for those seven years I have been searching. Searching everywhere.

Shakur   You don't have to be grateful. It is good you have found us. Now you can go back and be happy. You can tell your wife Altaaf is in a secure home.

Manohar Lal   Bhai, we want our son. If your son was lost, would you not want him back?

Shakur   He is emotionally attached to us. He's our son.

Manohar Lal   He is mine. My wife bore him. The blood that runs in his veins is mine. When his body turns to ashes, He will be flesh of my flesh.

Shakur   The azaan has been read in his ear. He goes to the mosque every Friday. He says his prayers five times a day.

Manohar Lal   I don't care if he has converted.

Shakur   Why uproot him now?

Manohar Lal   I'm not uprooting him. I'm taking him back to his roots.

Shakur   What makes you think he will go with you?

Manohar Lal   Ask him. Let me see him and ask him.

Shakur   You walked past him in the street.

Manohar Lal   Bhai sahib, you are a father. I accept that you have been his father but he is still my boy.

Shakur   Spare yourself, bhai sahib. He will not even recognise you.

Manohar Lal   I will take my chance.

Shakur   Altaaf beta. Idhar aana.

Altaaf *comes out with* **Zainab** *in purdah.*

Shakur   Beta salaam karo.

Pali   Asalaam walaikum.

Manohar Lal   Walaikum salaam.

(*Inner voice.*)
   He is my Pali,
   I know.
   That scar on his chin,
   When I pushed him high
   On the swing
   And he fell off.

Shakur   Beta, do you recognise this man?

Pali   Yes.

Shakur *is scared.* **Manohar Lal** *can't believe his luck.*

Pali   He asked us the way. You said he's from India.

Shakur   You see.

Manohar Lal (*taking out a photo*)   May I show him this?

Shakur *nods.*

Manohar Lal   Beta, do you remember the Baisakhi fair? This is my boy. This is my wife carrying baby Gudiya. This is me. Beta, do you remember your mother?

Pali (*in recognition*)   Pitaji, mataji, Gudiya.

Manohar Lal   Pali. My Pali!

Shakur   Beta. This is your real father. He has come for you. Do you want to go to India with him?

Pali   I want to stay with my ammi and abu.

Shakur   You heard the boy.

Manohar Lal   The law is on my side.

Shakur   We can drag the case on forever.

Manohar Lal (*pleading to* **Zainab**)   Sister, I am not begging you for my child, I'm begging you for my wife's life. She is like the living dead. The boy's absence has driven her insane. I cannot go back, having found him, but empty-handed. Day and night, she thinks of him. We have lost our baby girl.

Pali   Gudiya! What happened to our baby?

Manohar Lal   You remember Gudiya? Beta, she is beloved to God.

Pali   She's dead?

Manohar Lal   God had more need of her and called her. You are a mother, sister. Please take pity on my wife. She is like a bird whose nest has been destroyed.

Zainab (*affected by* **Manohar Lal**'s *plea*)   Take him. He is yours. Take him. I don't want to hurt an unfortunate woman.

Shakur   What are you saying, Zainab?

Zainab   If the child was ours and we had lost him, think how you would feel. It's a sin to keep a child from his own parents.

Manohar Lal   Sister, I will forever be in your debt.

Zainab   In my heart, I have always known he was another's wealth on loan to me. Each year that passed I would pray that the debt be written off and not be recalled.

Pause.

I will part with him on one condition. You must send him to us every year on Eid to stay with us for a month.

Manohar Lal   He is your wealth, bahen. You have my word.

Zainab   Come for him tomorrow. He will be ready.

Manohar Lal *leaves.*

Zainab   Mere soné, come here.

Pali *doesn't budge, clearly upset.*

Pali   You sending me away cos I'm bad.

Shakur   No beta. Who says you're bad?

Pali   I said you wasn't my family, and now you don't want me to be your family.

Zainab   You are our whole world.

Pali   Please don't let him take me.

Shakur   He is your pitaji, beta. The roots and tree from where you came.

Zainab   We were lucky to make you ours for a short time.

Pali   Please, ammi, don't send me.

Zainab   Your mataji is bereft without you and your sister. For seven years while you lit up our life, her life has been in darkness.

Pali *starts crying.*

Zainab   Cry. Let the ocean out.

Pali   I won't go. You can't make me. I'm not going.

He runs off.

Scene Sixteen

A little while later. **Buttameez***'s hideout. A barn or makeshift shelter.*

Buttameez   They'll be looking for you.

Pali I hate them. They want to send me away.

Buttameez To your real family.

Pali Who lost me. What makes them think they can get me back?

Buttameez At least you can get them back.

Pali I prayed and wished for him to come. Now I wish my wish hadn't come true.

Buttameez He's your dad. You lucky.

Pali I know he's my dad but he's not my abu. Is this where you sleep?

Buttameez Yeah.

Pali Cool!

Buttameez Cold you mean. Freezing in the winter.

Pali Can I stay here forever? No one tells you what to do.

Buttameez *is silent.*

Pali What happened to your family? You never said.

Buttameez I never told no one. Only the horses.

Pali Horses? What horses?

Buttameez The tonga wallahs let me groom their horses for two annas. They give me food and let me stay here.

Pali You can't speak to horses.

Buttameez I can. You have to whisper to them and they answer you back. I trust them and they trust me.

Pali You can trust me.

Buttameez You really wanna know?

Pali You know everything about me.

Buttameez *is hesitant as he tells his story.*

Buttameez All right then . . . First when the bullets started flying over our heads, it was pure fireworks . . . We'd play dodge ball but it was like real bullets . . . People said the white goras had drawn a line on the map and now the Muslims had to go to a new country . . . Pakistan. I didn't wanna go. Before we could leave the Hindu mob came . . . I recognised our neighbour and Guddu's dad . . . Guddu was like my best friend, you know . . . We traded bante and swam in the river . . . My dad was brave . . . he could like actually mash someone if they even said something about his family . . . but he just stood there . . . I saw them cut off his head and set fire to the house . . . I climbed to the roof and jumped into a pile of sugar cane skins. They didn't see me . . . my legs. I didn't feel the pain . . . I just hid there covered in sugar cane skins and licking them cos I was thirsty . . . my family burned inside . . . They were screamin' and that . . . At night, I started walking straight . . . could hardly stand . . . kept asking people . . . 'Where is Pakistan? Which way?' I saw Hasina sitting alone . . . I told her to walk with me. We crossed the border but we never saw no line.

Pali Can I stay here and be your family?

Buttameez No. I'm no one's family.

Pali Why didn't you get adopted?

Buttameez This old woman wanted me. She said her house was my house. I said I got no family, I don't need a house. And a schoolteacher said I could be his son but I didn't want to. I'm bad luck.

Pali It's not true. I always win if you're on my team.

Buttameez Don't want to love anyone else. If you love people you lose them.

Pali Or they lose you.

Buttameez *gives* **Pali** *back his mama kilti.*

Buttameez I dried this for you.

Pali Thanks.

He sniffs it.

Smells different. Of river water.

Scene Seventeen

The next day. Maidan.

Aisha *and* **Pali** *are hanging around the Maidan, messing around with their marbles or whatever.*

Aisha Just think, you'll get two lots of presents on your birthday. You'll celebrate Diwali and Eid . . .

Pali Easier to have one mum and dad.

Aisha Never even seen my dad.

Pali Who is he? You never said.

Aisha You never asked.

Pali So you gonna tell me? Last chance.

Aisha It's my ammi's secret. I'm a 'love child'. Special, she says, but I'd rather have a dad.

Pali You can have one of mine.

Aisha You might like your real mum and dad.

Pali I just want everything to stay the same. Friends. Family.

Aisha My ammi says nothing stays the same. Only her feelings.

Buttameez *and* **Pagal Head** *come with* **Hasina. Pagal Head** *gives him an old box of marbles.*

Pali My treasure of bante! From the hidey hole.

Pagal Head You can use them to mash up them Hindu vegetarians. They got no chance.

Buttameez   Remember when we made you eat chicken kebab and pretended it was paneer?

Pali   You tricked me.

Buttameez   But you pure love chicken now.

Pagal Head   You gonna get murghi in India?

Pali   Dunno.

Buttameez   Can't go back to being veggie. Muslims are strong.

Pali   And Hindus are clever.

Pagal Head   But they darpok innit? Cowards.

Pali   People are people.

Pagal Head *realises what he's said.*

Pagal Head   You come back on Eid and we suck the bones from the biryani.

They say goodbye. **Pali** *is left with* **Hasina**.

Hasina   Everyone was looking for you last night.

Pali   I ran away.

Hasina   But you came back.

Pali   Yeah. When are you going?

Hasina   Today. Same as you.

Pali   You takin' your shoes?

Hasina   No. They've fallen apart.

Pali   Give me a letter for your ammi. I'll deliver it to her when I'm in Delhi.

Hasina   No need.

Pali   I'll be in the same town. Don't you want me to find her?

Hasina The soft lady wrote to her. She sent her permission for me to be adopted.

Pali She knew where you were?

Hasina All this time. Said she can't take me back; that I belong here.

Pali Wonder where I belong?

Hasina People should belong to each other, not to places.

Pali I'm sorry.

Hasina Me too.

Pali I'll think about you really, really hard and maybe you'll think about me at the same time.

Hasina Maybe.

Pali You're the one who said.

Hasina Maybe I was wrong.

Pali I'll see you when I come back on Eid?

Hasina Yeah.

Scene Eighteen

Back in India.

Manohar Lal *and their friends are celebrating* **Pali**'*s return with a Punjabi festive song.* **Kaushalya** *is resplendent in a red chunri,* **Pali** *is withdrawn.*

Song

    Chita kukadh banerey tey x2
    Kasni dupattey valiye
    Munda aashik terey tey
    Gaddi aundiye tation tey x2
    Parey hath vay Babu
    Saanu maiya vekhan dey

Aalu matar pakaye hoye ney x2
Sadey nalon button changey
Jaiday seenay nal laaye hoye nay
Chita kukadh banerey tey x2
Kasni dupattey valiye
Munda aashik terey tey.

(*English translation for alternative.*)

[The white cockerel is on the rooftop
Oh girl with the sky-blue dupatta,
The boy is besotted with you.
The train is approaching the station
Get out of the way Babu,
Let me look at my beloved.
There are potatoes and peas cooked today
The buttons on your shirt are luckier than me,
As they are close to your heart.
The white cockerel is on the rooftop
Oh girl with the sky-blue dupatta
The boy is besotted with you.]

Woman   Who knows the ways of God, Kaushalya? The child you held safely to your bosom was snatched by death, and the child who strayed away has come back safe and sound.

Man   He's a lucky boy indeed to have had God's protection.

Woman   He's very quiet.

Kaushalya   So much has happened for him.

Pali *quietly gets his prayer mat, lays it down and starts to do his namaaz.*

Woman   What's going on, Kaushalya? What is your son doing?

Manohar Lal   He instinctively knows when it's time for namaaz.

Man   Why don't you stop him?

Kaushalya He's been through so much. He'll learn soon enough.

Man Manohar bhai, we don't want a Muslim amongst us.

Manohar Lal They were very good parents to him. They don't have a child of their own. It was natural for them to bring him up as a Muslim. What else could they do?

Woman Hai Ram! Have you thought, who will give him their girl if word gets out about all this?

Kaushalya I can't worry about his marriage just yet. I still have to win his heart.

Man *goes up to* **Pali**.

Man What were you doing?

Pali I was saying my namaaz.

Man We won't allow you to do this thing here. From today, no namaaz, you understand?

Kaushalya He's only a child, leave him.

Man Manohar Lal, better call a pandit and a barber. We need to shave his head and make him pure again. Undo this conversion.

Manohar Lal All in good time, bhai, let him adjust to his circumstances.

Man You will regret it if you wait a minute longer.

Manohar Lal There's too much emphasis placed on these things.

Man You don't care that your son has come back as a Muslim?

Manohar Lal It is enough for me that my son has come back.

Man I can't believe my ears. What is your name, boy?

Pali   Altaaf.

Man   No, your name is Pali. Who told you your name is Altaaf?

Pali   My abbaji.

Man   Abbaji. This is your pitaji. Repeat your name five times; Pali, Pali . . . Pali.

Manohar Lal   Please. I will not let you frighten my boy.

Man   Either sort him out or send him back to those Muslims. We won't tolerate this here. (*To* **Woman**.) Chalo.

Woman   Might have been better if he had never been found.

Man *and* **Woman** *leave.*

Manohar Lal (*inner voice*)
  I live among them,
  But these are not my people.
  My people
  Cared not for Bhagwan or Allah.
  They shared
  Love and lassi,
  In each other's homes.
  What happened then
  To cause this narrowing of minds,
  And the broadening
  Of this divide?

Pali   I was only doing my prayers.

Kaushalya   I know, but we pray in a different way. We'll teach you to pray our way and we'll call you Pali again.

Pali   But that's not my name.

He starts crying.

Manohar Lal   Even our hearts are left across the border, beta. This place will never be home.

Kaushalya   We have had to start again and try to belong.

Pali   People should belong to each other and not to places.

Manohar Lal   Yes, you are right, and we are family.

Kaushalya   When Gudiya was born and you were jealous, you remember you would run to me and lie on my stomach? I would wrap my dupatta over you and you would pretend that you were a baby growing inside me. You came from me, beta, and now you've come back to me.

Pali *goes into her arms. The beginning of reconnection.*

Scene Nineteen

Back in Pakistan. **Shakur** *and* **Zainab**'s *home.*

Zainab   He's gone and with him has gone all the gaiety of this house. This time of night I would be searching the streets for him. He would hide and try to snatch more time with his friends. I would never know where to find him.

Shakur   Now even his friends have dispersed.

Zainab   What do you think? Will he come to visit us on Eid? Will those people send him?

Shakur   He looked like a man of his word.

Zainab   Yes. Inshallah, we will see him again.

She starts to cry.

Shakur   Cry. Let the ocean out.

End on soundtrack of children singing 'Lab pe aati hai dua bankey tamanna meri', a prayer about the hope that children offer, by the poet Iqbal.

The End